Your Prayers

A Guidebook to a More Powerful Prayer Life

BARBOUR
PUBLISHING

Published by Barbour Publishing, Inc., P.O. Box 719, Uhrichsville, Ohio 44683, www.barbourbooks.com

Our mission is to publish and distribute inspirational products offering exceptional value and biblical encouragement to the masses.

Member of the
Evangelical Christian
Publishers Association

Printed in the United States of America.

CONTENTS

INTRODUCTION

What would you tell someone if he or she were to approach you and ask, "How should I pray?" Would you recommend times and places to "get alone with God"? Or would you recommend the person kneel or stand or raise his or her hands?

When it comes to prayer, those aren't bad things to talk about. But prayer is so much more than where we do it or what physical posture we take. It's a whole lot more than telling God what you want.

Someone once said that praying is as natural to a human as breathing. And yet so few of us really know *how* to do it— at least in the way that God says to do it. In fact, the people who were the closest to Jesus—His twelve apostles—didn't have a clue how they should pray. That's why they asked Him one day, "Lord, teach us to pray!"

That's what this book is all about.

Here, under one cover, are three popular books on prayer:

1. ***A 31-Day Guide to Prayer,*** a century-old classic by Andrew Murray, one of the world's leading authorities on the deeper Christian life. This brief, easy-to-understand guide provides a month's worth of insight on both *what* to pray for and *how* to pray. Relevant scriptures and Murray's devotional thoughts encourage you to take the steps necessary to commit to actual praying.

2. ***Prayer Vitals,*** a compilation of facts and figures, goals and guidance regarding prayer. In this section, you'll find some biblical what's, how's, and where's of prayer; the five different ways God want you to talk to Him; thirty biblical prayers to remember; Jesus' teaching and example on prayer; some great saying about prayer; and much more.

3. *Prayers & Promises,* an encouraging collection of topical "prayer starters," each accompanied by a scriptural promise from God.

Though we do hope you enjoy reading it, this book much more than just an interesting collection of information. It's meant to challenge you, to get you thinking about what it really means to pray.

You won't come away from this book knowing all there is to know about prayer. No book this size will even begin to scratch the surface of that subject. But you'll have a pretty good idea of what the Bible really says about prayer—what you should pray, what you can pray for, and how you can best pray those prayers.

This powerful book will start you on a journey of prayer that can truly change your life!

A 31-DAY GUIDE TO PRAYER

Andrew Murray

Introduction

Prayer, in its simplest definition, is talking with God. It can cover the entire range of human experience and emotion, and God is pleased to listen whatever our topic may be. But in His Word, the Bible, God has also provided some very specific instruction for prayer.

The great Christian theologian, Andrew Murray, has created the following thirty-one-day guide to prayer, providing timeless guidance that will enable readers to have vital, truly biblical prayer lives of their own. The indispensable wisdom in the book will lead you to a closer relationship with God and His Son, Jesus Christ.

Read on for a biblical framework for prayer. Put these words into practice, and experience the power of prayer in your world.

PRAY WITHOUT CEASING

Pray without ceasing. Who can do this? How can one do it who is surrounded by the cares of daily life? How can a mother love her child without ceasing? How can the eyelid without ceasing hold itself ready to protect the eye? How can I breathe and feel and hear without ceasing? Because all these are the functions of a healthy, natural life. And so, if the spiritual life be healthy, under the full power of the Holy Spirit, praying without ceasing will be natural.

Pray without ceasing. Does it refer to continual acts of prayer, in which we are to persevere till we obtain, or to the spirit of prayerfulness that should animate us all the day? It includes both. The example of our Lord Jesus shows us this. We have to enter our closet for special seasons of prayer; we are at times to persevere there in importunate prayer. We are also all the day to walk in God's presence, with the whole heart set upon heavenly things. Without set times of prayer, the spirit of prayer will be dull and feeble. Without the continual prayerfulness, the set times will not avail.

Pray without ceasing. Does that refer to prayer for ourselves or others? To both. It is because many confine it to themselves that they fail so in practicing it. It is only when the branch gives itself to bear fruit, more fruit, much fruit, that it can live a healthy life and expect a rich inflow of sap. The death of Christ brought Him to the place of everlasting intercession. Your death with Him to sin and self sets you free from the care of self and elevates you to the dignity of intercessor—one who can get life and blessing from God for others. Know your calling; begin this your work. Give yourself wholly to it, and ere you know, you will be finding something of this *"praying always"* within you.

Pray without ceasing. How can I learn it? The best way of learning to do a thing—in fact the only way—is *to do it*. Begin by setting apart some time every day, say ten or fifteen minutes, in which you say to God and to yourself that you come to Him now as intercessor for others. Let it be after your morning or evening prayer, or any other time. If you cannot secure the same time every day, be not troubled. Only see that you do your work. Christ chose you and appointed you to pray for others.

If at first you do not feel any special urgency or faith or power in your prayers, let not that hinder you. Quietly tell your Lord Jesus of your feebleness; believe that the Holy Spirit is in you to teach you to pray, and be assured that if you begin, God will help you. God cannot help you unless you begin and keep on.

Pray without ceasing. How do I know what to pray for? If once you begin and think of all the needs around, you will soon find enough. But to help you, this little tract is issued, with subjects and hints for prayer for a month. It is meant that we should use it month by month, until we know more fully to follow the Spirit's leading, and have learned, if need be, to make our own list of subjects, and can dispense with it. In regard to the use of these helps, a few words may be needed.

1. How to pray. You notice for every day two headings—the one *What to Pray;* the other, *How to Pray.* If the subjects were only given, one might fall into the routine of mentioning names and things before God, and the work becomes a burden. The hints under the heading *How to Pray* are meant to remind of the spiritual nature of the work, of the need of divine help, and to encourage faith in the certainty that God, through the Spirit, will give us grace to pray aright and will also hear our prayer. One does not at once learn to take his place boldly and to dare to believe that he will be heard. Therefore take a few moments each day to listen to God's voice reminding you of how certainly even you will be heard, and calling on you to pray in that faith in your Father to claim and take the blessing you plead for. And let these words about how to pray enter your hearts and occupy your thoughts at other times, too. The work of intercession is Christ's great work on earth, entrusted to Him because He gave Himself the sacrifice to God for men, and the work will become your glory and your joy, too.

2. What to pray. Scripture calls us to pray for many things: for all saints; for all men; for kings and all rulers; for all who are in adversity; for the sending forth of laborers; for those who labor in the gospel; for all converts; for believers who have fallen into sin; for one another in our own immediate circles. The church is now so much larger than when the New Testament was written; the number of forms of work and workers is so much greater, the needs of the church and the world are so much better known, that we need to take time and thought to see where prayer is needed and to what our heart is most drawn out. The Scripture calls to prayer demand a large heart, taking in all saints and all men and all needs. An attempt has been made in these helps to indicate what the chief subjects are that need prayer and that ought to interest every Christian.

It will be felt difficult by many to pray for such large spheres as are sometimes mentioned. Let it be understood that in each case we may make special intercession for our own circle of interest coming under that heading. And it is hardly needful to say, further, that where one subject appears of more special interest or urgency than another we are free for a time day after day to take up that subject. If only time be really given to intercession, and the spirit of believing intercession be cultivated, the object is attained. While on the one hand the heart must be enlarged at times to take in all, the more pointed and definite our prayer can be, the better.

3. Answers to prayer. More than one little book has been published in which Christians may keep a register of their petitions and note when they were answered. When we pray for all saints or for missions in general, it is difficult to know when or how our prayer is answered, or whether our prayer has had any part in bringing the answer. It is of extreme importance that we should prove that God hears us, and to this end take note of what answers we look for and when they come. On the day of praying for all saints, take the saints in your congregation, or in your prayer meeting, and ask for a revival among them. Take, in connection with missions, some special station or missionary you are interested in, or more than one, and plead for blessing. And expect and look for its coming that you may praise God.

4. Prayer circles. There is no desire in publishing this invitation to intercession to add another to the many existing prayer unions or praying bands. The first object is to stir the many Christians who practically, through ignorance of their calling or unbelief as to their prayer availing much, take but very little part in the work of intercession; and then to help those who do pray to some fuller apprehension of the greatness of the work and the need of giving their whole strength to it. There is a circle of prayer which asks for prayer on the first day of every month for the fuller manifestation of the power of the Holy Spirit throughout the church. I have given the words of that invitation as subject for the first day, and taken the same thought as keynote all through. The more one thinks of the need and the promise and the greatness of the obstacles to be overcome in prayer, the more one feels it must become our lifework day by day, that to which every other interest is subordinated.

But while not forming a large prayer union, it is suggested that it may be found helpful to have small prayer circles to unite in prayer, either for one month, with some special object introduced daily along with the others, or through a year or longer, with the view of strengthening each other in the grace of intercession. If a minister were to invite some of his neighboring brethren to join for some special requests along with the printed subjects for supplication, or a number of the more earnest members of his congregation to unite in prayer for revival, some might be trained to take their place in the great work of intercession, who now stand idle because no man hath hired them.

5. Who is sufficient for these things? The more we study and try to practice this grace of intercession, the more we become overwhelmed by its greatness and our feebleness. Let every such impression lead us to listen: My grace is sufficient for thee and to answer truthfully: Our sufficiency is of God. Take courage; it is in the intercession of Christ you are called to take part. The burden and the agony, the triumph and the victory are all His. Learn from Him, yield to His Spirit in you to know how to pray. He gave Himself a sacrifice to God for men that He might have the right and power of intercession. "He bare the sin of many, and made intercession for the transgressors." Let your faith rest boldly on His finished work. Let your heart wholly identify itself with Him in His death and His life. **Like Him,** give yourself to God a sacrifice for men: It is your highest nobility; it is your true and full union to Him; it will be to you, as to Him, your power of intercession. Beloved Christian! Come and give your whole heart and life to intercession, and you will know its blessedness and its power. God asks nothing less; the world needs nothing less; Christ asks nothing less; let nothing less be what we offer to God.

Day One

WHAT TO PRAY:
For the Power of the Holy Spirit

I bow my knees unto the Father. . .
that he would grant you. . .
to be strengthened with might by his Spirit.
Ephesians 3:14, 16

Wait for the promise of the Father.
Acts 1:4

The fuller manifestation of the grace and energy of the blessed Spirit of God, in the removal of all that is contrary to God's revealed will, so that we grieve not the Holy Spirit, but that He may work in mightier power in the church for the exaltation of Christ and the blessing of souls.

God has one promise to and through His exalted Son; our Lord has one gift to His church; the church has one need; all prayer unites in the one petition—the power of the Holy Spirit. Make it your one prayer.

Special Petitions

_____

_____

_____

_____

_____

HOW TO PRAY:
As a Child Asks a Father

> *If a son shall ask bread of any of you that*
> *is a father, will he give him a stone? . . .*
> *How much more shall your heavenly Father*
> *give the Holy Spirit to them that ask him?*
> Luke 11:11, 13

Ask as simply and trustfully as a child asks bread. You can do this because "God hath sent forth the Spirit of his Son into your hearts, crying, Abba, Father." This Spirit is in you to give you childlike confidence. In the faith of His praying in you, ask for the power of that Holy Spirit everywhere. Mention places or circles where you specially ask it to be seen.

Special Petitions

_____

_____

_____

_____

_____

Day Two

WHAT TO PRAY:
FOR THE SPIRIT OF SUPPLICATION

The Spirit itself maketh intercession for us.
ROMANS 8:26

I will pour [out]. . .the spirit of. . .supplications.
ZECHARIAH 12:10

Every child of God has the Holy Spirit in him to pray. God waits to give the Spirit in full measure. Ask for yourself, and all who join, the outpouring of the Spirit of supplication. Ask it for your own prayer circle.

SPECIAL PETITIONS

_____

_____

_____

_____

_____

HOW TO PRAY:
IN THE SPIRIT

*Praying always with all prayer
and supplication in the Spirit.*
EPHESIANS 6:18

Praying in the Holy Ghost.
JUDE 20

Our Lord gave His disciples on His resurrection day the Holy Spirit to enable them to wait for the full outpouring on the day of Pentecost. It is only in the power of the Spirit already in us, acknowledged and yielded to, that we can pray for His fuller manifestation. Say to the Father, it is the Spirit of His Son in you that is urging you to plead His promise.

SPECIAL PETITIONS

Day Three

WHAT TO PRAY:
For all Saints

With all prayer and supplication in the Spirit,
and watching thereunto with all perseverance
and supplication for all saints.
Ephesians 6:18

Every member of a body is interested in the welfare of the whole and exists to help and complete the others. Believers are one body and ought to pray, not so much for the welfare of their own church or society, but, first of all, for all saints. This large, unselfish love is the proof that Christ's Spirit and love are teaching them to pray. Pray first for all and then for the believers around you.

Special Petitions

_____

_____

_____

_____

_____

HOW TO PRAY:
In the Love of the Spirit

> *By this shall all men know*
> *that ye are my disciples,*
> *if ye have love one to another.*
> John 13:35

> *[I pray]. . .that they all may be one. . .*
> *that the world may believe*
> *that thou hast sent me.*
> John 17:20–21

> *I beseech you, brethren. . .*
> *for the love of the Spirit,*
> *that ye strive together with me*
> *in your prayers to God for me.*
> Romans 15:30

> *Above all things have fervent charity*
> *among yourselves.*
> 1 Peter 4:8

If we are to pray, we must love. Let us say to God we do love all His saints; let us say we love specially every child of His we know. Let us pray with fervent love, in the love of the Spirit.

Special Petitions

_____

_____

_____

_____

_____

Day Four

WHAT TO PRAY:
For the Spirit of Holiness

God is the holy One. His people is a holy people. He speaks: I am holy: I am the Lord who makes you holy. Christ prayed: Sanctify them. Make them holy through Thy truth. Paul prayed: "[God] stablish your hearts unblameable in holiness." God of peace, sanctify you wholly!

Pray for all saints—God's holy ones—throughout the church that the Spirit of holiness may rule them. Specially for new converts. For the saints in your own neighborhood or congregation. For any you are specially interested in. Think of their special need, weakness, or sin; and pray that God may make them holy.

Special Petitions

_____

_____

_____

_____

_____

HOW TO PRAY:
TRUSTING IN GOD'S OMNIPOTENCE

The things that are impossible with men are possible with God. When we think of the great things we ask for, of how little likelihood there is of their coming, of our own insignificance—prayer is not only wishing or asking, but believing and accepting. Be still before God and ask Him to give you to know Him as the almighty One, and leave your petitions with Him who doeth wonders.

SPECIAL PETITIONS

_____

_____

_____

_____

_____

DAY FIVE

WHAT TO PRAY:
THAT GOD'S PEOPLE MAY BE KEPT FROM THE WORLD

Holy Father, keep through thine own name
those whom thou hast given me. . . .
I pray not that thou shouldest
take them out of the world,
but that thou shouldest keep them from the evil.
They are not of the world, even as I am not of the world.
JOHN 17:11, 15–16

In the last night, Christ asked three things for His disciples: that they might be kept as those who are not of the world; that they might be sanctified; that they might be one in love. You cannot do better than pray as Jesus prayed. Ask for God's people that they may be kept separate from the world and its spirit; that they, by the Holy Spirit, may live as those who are not of the world.

SPECIAL PETITIONS

_____

_____

_____

_____

_____

HOW TO PRAY:
HAVING CONFIDENCE BEFORE GOD

> *Beloved, if our heart condemn us not,*
> *then have we confidence*
> *toward God. And whatsoever we ask,*
> *we receive of him,*
> *because we keep his commandments,*
> *and do those things that are pleasing in his sight.*
> 1 JOHN 3:21–22

Learn these words by heart. Get them into your heart. Join the ranks of those who, with John, draw nigh to God with an assured heart that does not condemn them, having confidence toward God. In this spirit, pray for your brother who sins (1 John 5:16). In the quiet confidence of an obedient child, plead for those of your brethren who may be giving way to sin. Pray for all to be kept from the evil. And say often, "What we ask, we receive, because we keep and do."

SPECIAL PETITIONS

_____

_____

_____

_____

_____

Day Six

WHAT TO PRAY:
For the Spirit of Love in the Church

[I pray] that they may be one, even as we are one:
I in them, and thou in me. . .that the world may know
that thou hast sent me, and hast loved them,
as thou hast loved me. . . . That the love wherewith
thou hast loved me may be in them, and I in them.
John 17:22–23, 26

The fruit of the Spirit is love.
Galatians 5:22

Believers are one in Christ, as He is one with the Father. The love of God rests on them and can dwell in them. Pray that the power of the Holy Ghost may work this love in believers, that the world may see and know God's love in them. Pray much for this.

Special Petitions

_____

_____

_____

_____

_____

HOW TO PRAY:
AS ONE OF GOD'S REMEMBRANCERS

I have set watchmen upon thy walls. . .
which shall never hold their peace day nor night:
ye that make mention of the Lord keep not silence,
and give him no rest.
ISAIAH 62:6–7

Study these words until your whole soul be filled with the consciousness: I am appointed intercessor. Enter God's presence in that faith. Study the world's need with that thought—it is my work to intercede; the Holy Spirit will teach me for what and how. Let it be an abiding consciousness: My great lifework, like Christ's, is intercession—to pray for believers and those who do not yet know God.

SPECIAL PETITIONS

_____

_____

_____

_____

_____

Day Seven

WHAT TO PRAY:
For the Power of the Holy Spirit on Ministers

I beseech you. . .
that ye strive together with me
in your prayers to God for me.
Romans 15:30

He will yet deliver us;
ye also helping together by prayer. . .
on our behalf.
2 Corinthians 1:10–11

What a great host of ministers there are in Christ's church. What need they have of prayer. What a power they might be if they were all clothed with the power of the Holy Ghost. Pray definitely for this; long for it. Think of your own minister, and ask it very specially for him. Connect every thought of the ministry, in your town or neighborhood or the world, with the prayer that all may be filled with the Spirit. Plead for them the promise, "Tarry. . .until ye be endued with power from on high." "Ye shall receive power, after that the Holy Ghost is come upon you."

Special Petitions

_____

_____

_____

_____

_____

HOW TO PRAY:
In Secret

> *But thou, when thou prayest,*
> *enter into thy closet,*
> *and when thou hast shut thy door,*
> *pray to thy Father which is in secret.*
> MATTHEW 6:6

> *He went up into a mountain*
> *apart to pray. . .he was there alone.*
> MATTHEW 14:23; SEE ALSO JOHN 6:15

Take time and realize, when you are alone with God: Here am I now, face-to-face with God, to intercede for His servants. Do not think you have no influence or that your prayer will be missed. Your prayer and faith will make a difference. Cry in secret to God for His ministers.

Special Petitions

_____

_____

_____

_____

_____

DAY EIGHT

WHAT TO PRAY:
FOR THE SPIRIT ON
ALL CHRISTIAN WORKERS

Ye also helping together by prayer for us,
that for the gift bestowed upon us
by the means of many persons
thanks may be given by many on our behalf.
2 CORINTHIANS 1:11

What multitudes of workers in connection with our churches and missions, our railways and postmen, our soldiers and sailors, our young men and young women, our fallen men and women, our poor and sick. God be praised for this! What could they accomplish if each were living in the fullness of the Holy Spirit! Pray for them; it makes you a partner in their work, and you will praise God each time you hear of blessing anywhere.

SPECIAL PETITIONS

_____

_____

_____

_____

_____

HOW TO PRAY:
With Definite Petitions

What wilt thou that I shall do unto thee?
Luke 18:41

The Lord knew what the man wanted, and yet He asked him. The utterance of our wish gives point to the transaction in which we are engaged with God, and so awakens faith and expectation. Be very definite in your petitions, so as to know what answer you may look for. Just think of the great host of workers, and ask and expect God definitely to bless them in answer to the prayers of His people. Then ask still more definitely for workers around you. Intercession is not the breathing out of pious wishes; its aim is, in believing, persevering prayer, to receive and bring down blessing.

Special Petitions

_____

_____

_____

_____

_____

DAY NINE

WHAT TO PRAY:
FOR GOD'S SPIRIT ON OUR MISSION WORK

As they ministered to the Lord, and fasted,
the Holy Ghost said,
Separate me Barnabas and Saul. . . .
When they had fasted and prayed. . .
they sent them away.
So they, being sent forth by the Holy Ghost, departed.

ACTS 13:2–4

The evangelization of the world depends first of all upon a revival of prayer. Deeper than the need for men—aye, deep down at the bottom of our spiritless life, is the need for the forgotten secret of prevailing, worldwide prayer.

Pray that our mission work may all be done in this spirit—waiting on God, hearing the voice of the Spirit, sending forth men with fasting and prayer. Pray that in our churches our mission interest and mission work may be in the power of the Holy Spirit and of prayer. It is a Spirit-filled, praying church that will send out Spirit-filled missionaries, mighty in prayer.

SPECIAL PETITIONS

_____

_____

_____

_____

_____

HOW TO PRAY:
Take Time

I give myself unto prayer.
PSALM 109:4

We will give ourselves continually to prayer.
ACTS 6:4

Be not rash with thy mouth,
and let not thine heart
be hasty to utter any thing before God.
ECCLESIASTES 5:2

And [He] continued all night
in prayer to God.
LUKE 6:12

Time is one of the chief standards of value. The time we give is a proof of the interest we feel.

We need time with God—to realize His presence; to wait for Him to make Himself known; to consider and feel the needs we plead for; to take our place in Christ; to pray 'til we can believe that we have received. Take time in prayer, and pray down blessing on the mission work of the church.

Special Petitions

_____

_____

_____

_____

_____

Day Ten

WHAT TO PRAY:
For God's Spirit on Our Missionaries

Ye shall receive power,
after that the Holy Ghost is come upon you:
and ye shall be witnesses unto me. . .
unto the uttermost part of the earth.
ACTS 1:8

What the world needs today is not only more missionaries but the outpouring of God's Spirit on everyone whom He has sent out to work for Him in the foreign field.

God always gives His servants power equal to the work He asks of them. Think of the greatness and difficulty of this work—casting Satan out of his strongholds—and pray that everyone who takes part in it may receive and do all his work in the power of the Holy Ghost. Think of the difficulties of your missionaries, and pray for them.

Special Petitions

_____

_____

_____

_____

_____

HOW TO PRAY:
TRUSTING GOD'S FAITHFULNESS

He is faithful that promised. . . .
She judged him faithful who had promised.
HEBREWS 10:23; 11:11

J ust think of God's promises to His Son, concerning His kingdom; to the church, concerning the heathen; to His servants, concerning their work; to yourself, concerning your prayer; and pray in the assurance that He is faithful and only waits for prayer and faith to fulfill them. "Faithful is he that calleth you" (to pray), "who also will do it" (what He has promised) (1 Thess. 5:24).

Take up individual missionaries, make yourself one with them, and pray 'til you know that you are heard. Oh, begin to live for Christ's kingdom as the one thing worth living for!

SPECIAL PETITIONS

_____

_____

_____

_____

_____

DAY ELEVEN

WHAT TO PRAY:
FOR MORE LABORERS

Pray ye therefore the Lord of the harvest,
that he will send forth labourers into his harvest.
MATTHEW 9:38

What a remarkable call of the Lord Jesus for help from His disciples in getting the need supplied. What an honor put upon prayer. What a proof that God wants prayer and will hear it.

Pray for laborers, for all students in theological seminaries, training homes, Bible institutes, that they may not go unless He fits them and sends them forth; that our churches may train their students to seek for the sending forth of the Holy Spirit; that all believers may hold themselves ready to be sent forth, or to pray for those who can go.

SPECIAL PETITIONS

_____

_____

_____

_____

_____

HOW TO PRAY:
In Faith, Nothing Doubting

Jesus answering saith unto them,
Have faith in God. . . .
Whosoever shall say unto this mountain,
Be thou removed, and be thou cast into the sea;
and shall not doubt in his heart, but shall believe that. . .
which he saith shall come to pass; he shall have [it].
MARK 11:22–23

Have faith in God! Ask Him to make Himself known to you as the faithful, mighty God, who worketh all in all; and you will be encouraged to believe that He can give suitable and sufficient laborers, however impossible this appears. But, remember, in answer to prayer and faith.

Apply this to every opening where a good worker is needed. The work is God's. He can give the right workman. But He must be asked and waited on.

Special Petitions

_____

_____

_____

_____

_____

DAY TWELVE

WHAT TO PRAY:
FOR THE SPIRIT TO CONVINCE THE WORLD OF SIN

I will send [the Comforter] unto you.
And when he is come,
he will reprove the world of sin.
JOHN 16:7–8

God's one desire, the one object of Christ's being manifested, is to take away sin. The first work of the Spirit on the world is conviction of sin. Without that, there is no deep or abiding revival, no powerful conversion. Pray for it, that the gospel may be preached in such power of the Spirit, that men may see that they have rejected and crucified Christ and cry out, "What shall we do?"

Pray most earnestly for a mighty power of conviction of sin wherever the gospel is preached.

SPECIAL PETITIONS

_____

_____

_____

_____

_____

HOW TO PRAY:
STIR UP YOURSELF TO TAKE HOLD OF GOD'S STRENGTH

> *Let him take hold of my strength,*
> *that he may make peace with me.*
> ISAIAH 27:5

> *There is none that calleth upon thy name,*
> *that stirreth up himself*
> *to take hold of thee.*
> ISAIAH 64:7

> *Stir up the gift of God, which is in thee.*
> 2 TIMOTHY 1:6

First, take hold of God's strength. God is a Spirit. I cannot take hold of Him and hold Him fast but by the Spirit. Take hold of God's strength, and hold on 'til it has done for you what He has promised. Pray for the power of the Spirit to convict of sin.

Second, stir up yourself, the power that is in you by the Holy Spirit, to take hold. Give your whole heart and will to it, and say, I will not let Thee go except Thou bless me.

SPECIAL PETITIONS

_____

_____

_____

_____

_____

Day Thirteen

WHAT TO PRAY:
For the Spirit of Burning

And it shall come to pass,
that he that is left in Zion. . .shall be called holy. . .
when the Lord shall have washed away
the filth of the daughters of Zion. . .by the spirit
of judgment, and by the spirit of burning.
Isaiah 4:3–4

A washing by fire! A cleansing by judgment! He that has passed through this shall be called holy. The power of blessing for the world, the power of work and intercession that will avail, depends upon the spiritual state of the church; and that can only rise higher as sin is discovered and put away. Judgment must begin at the house of God. There must be conviction of sin for sanctification. Beseech God to give His Spirit as a spirit of judgment and a spirit of burning—to discover and burn out sin in His people.

Special Petitions

_____

_____

_____

_____

_____

HOW TO PRAY:
IN THE NAME OF CHRIST

Whatsoever ye shall ask in my name,
that will I do. . . .
If ye shall ask any thing in my name,
I will do it.
JOHN 14:13–14

Ask in the name of your redeemer God, who sits upon the throne. Ask what He has promised, what He gave His blood for, that sin may be put away from among His people. Ask—the prayer is after His own heart—for the spirit of deep conviction of sin to come among His people. Ask for the spirit of burning. Ask in the faith of His name—the faith of what He wills, of what He can do—and look for the answer. Pray that the church may be blessed, to be made a blessing in the world.

SPECIAL PETITIONS

_____

_____

_____

_____

_____

Day Fourteen

WHAT TO PRAY:
For the Church of the Future

[That the children] might not be as their fathers. . .
a generation that set not their heart aright,
and whose spirit was not stedfast with God.
Psalm 78:8

I will pour my spirit upon thy seed,
and my blessing upon thine offspring.
Isaiah 44:3

Pray for the rising generation who are to come after us. Think of the young men and young women and children of this age, and pray for all the agencies at work among them; that in associations and societies and unions, in homes and schools, Christ may be honored and the Holy Spirit get possession of them. Pray for the young of your own neighborhood.

Special Petitions

_____

_____

_____

_____

_____

HOW TO PRAY:
WITH THE WHOLE HEART

*The LORD. . .grant thee according
to thine own heart.*
PSALM 20:1, 4

Thou hast given him his heart's desire.
PSALM 21:2

*I cried with my whole heart; hear me,
O LORD.*
PSALM 119:145

God lives and listens to every petition with His whole heart. Each time we pray, the whole infinite God is there to hear. He asks that in each prayer the whole man shall be there, too; that we shall cry with our whole heart. Christ gave Himself to God for men; and so He takes up every need into His intercession. If once we seek God with our whole heart, the whole heart will be in every prayer with which we come to this God. Pray with your whole heart for the young.

SPECIAL PETITIONS

_____

_____

_____

_____

_____

Day Fifteen

WHAT TO PRAY:
For Schools and Colleges

As for me, this is my covenant with them,
saith the LORD; My spirit that is upon thee,
and my words which I have put in thy mouth,
shall not depart out of thy mouth,
nor out of the mouth of thy seed,
nor out of the mouth of thy seed's seed,
saith the LORD, from henceforth and for ever.
ISAIAH 59:21

The future of the church and the world depends, to an extent we little conceive, on the education of the day. The church may be seeking to evangelize the heathen and be giving up her own children to secular and materialistic influences. Pray for schools and colleges, and that the church may realize and fulfill its momentous duty of caring for its children. Pray for godly teachers.

Special Petitions

_____

_____

_____

_____

_____

HOW TO PRAY:
Not Limiting God

> *They. . .limited the Holy One of Israel.*
> PSALM 78:41

> *He did not many mighty works there
> because of their unbelief.*
> MATTHEW 13:58

> *Is any thing too hard for the LORD?*
> GENESIS 18:14

> *Ah Lord GOD! behold, thou hast made the heaven
> and the earth by thy great power. . .
> there is nothing too hard for thee. . . .
> Behold, I am the LORD. . .
> is there any thing too hard for me?*
> JEREMIAH 32:17, 27

Beware, in your prayer, above everything, of limiting God, not only by unbelief, but by fancying that you know what He can do. Expect unexpected things above all that we ask or think. Each time you intercede, be quiet first and worship God in His glory. Think of what He can do, of how He delights to hear Christ, of your place in Christ; and expect great things.

Special Petitions

_____

_____

_____

_____

_____

Day Sixteen

WHAT TO PRAY:
For the Power of the Holy Spirit in Our Sabbath Schools

Thus saith the LORD,
Even the captives of the mighty shall be taken away,
and the prey of the terrible shall be delivered:
for I will contend with him that contendeth
with thee, and I will save thy children.
ISAIAH 49:25

Every part of the work of God's church is His work. He must do it. Prayer is the confession that He will, the surrender of ourselves into His hands to let Him work in us and through us. Pray for the hundreds of thousands of Sunday school teachers, that those who know God may be filled with His Spirit. Pray for your own Sunday school. Pray for the salvation of the children.

Special Petitions

_____

_____

_____

_____

_____

HOW TO PRAY:
BOLDLY

*We have a great high priest. . .
Jesus the Son of God. . . .
Let us therefore come boldly
unto the throne of grace.*
HEBREWS 4:14, 16

These hints to help us in our work of intercession—what are they doing for us? Making us conscious of our feebleness in prayer? Thank God for this. It is the very first lesson we need on the way to pray the effectual prayer that availeth much. Let us persevere, taking each subject boldly to the throne of grace. As we pray we shall learn to pray and to believe and to expect with increasing boldness. Hold fast your assurance: It is at God's command you come as an intercessor. Christ will give you grace to pray aright.

SPECIAL PETITIONS

_____

_____

_____

_____

_____

Day Seventeen

WHAT TO PRAY:
For Kings and Rulers

I exhort therefore, that, first of all, supplications,
prayers, intercessions, giving of thanks,
be made for all men; for kings, and for all
that are in authority; that we may lead a quiet
and peaceable life in all godliness and honesty.
1 Timothy 2:1–2

What a faith in the power of prayer! A few feeble and despised Christians are to influence the mighty Roman emperors and help in securing peace and quietness. Let us believe that prayer is a power that is taken up by God in His rule of the world. Let us pray for our country and its rulers; for all the rulers of the world; for rulers in cities or districts in which we are interested. When God's people unite in this, they may count upon their prayer effecting in the unseen world more than they know. Let faith hold this fast.

Special Petitions

_____
_____
_____
_____
_____

HOW TO PRAY:
The Prayer before God as Incense

*And another angel came and stood at the altar,
having a golden censer;
and there was given unto him much incense,
that he should offer it with the prayers
of all saints upon the golden altar
which was before the throne.
And the smoke of the incense,
which came with the prayers of the saints,
ascended up before God out of the angel's hand.
And the angel took the censer,
and filled it with fire of the altar,
and cast it into the earth:
and there were voices, and thunderings,
and lightnings, and an earthquake.*
REVELATION 8:3–5

The same censer brings the prayer of the saints before God and casts fire upon the earth. The prayers that go up to heaven have their share in the history of this earth. Be sure that thy prayers enter God's presence.

Special Petitions

_____

_____

_____

_____

_____

DAY EIGHTEEN

WHAT TO PRAY:
FOR PEACE

*I exhort therefore, that, first of all, supplications. . .
be made. . .for kings, and for all that are in
authority; that we may lead a quiet and peaceable
life in all godliness and honesty. For this is good
and acceptable in the sight of God our Saviour.*
1 TIMOTHY 2:1–3

He maketh wars to cease unto the end of the earth.
PSALM 46:9

What a terrible sight!—the military armaments in which the nations find their pride. What a terrible thought!—the evil passions that may at any moment bring on war. And what a prospect the suffering and desolation that must come. God can, in answer to the prayer of His people, give peace. Let us pray for it and for the rule of righteousness on which alone it can be stablished.

SPECIAL PETITIONS

_____

_____

_____

_____

_____

HOW TO PRAY:
WITH THE UNDERSTANDING

What is it then?
I will pray with the spirit,
and I will pray with the understanding.
1 CORINTHIANS 14:15

We need to pray with the spirit, as the vehicle of the intercession of God's Spirit, if we are to take hold of God in faith and power. We need to pray with the understanding, if we are really to enter deeply into the needs we bring before Him. Take time to apprehend intelligently, in each subject, the nature, the extent, the urgency of the request, the ground and way and certainty of God's promise as revealed in His Word. Let the mind affect the heart. Pray with the understanding and with the spirit.

SPECIAL PETITIONS

_____

_____

_____

_____

_____

DAY NINETEEN

WHAT TO PRAY:
FOR THE HOLY SPIRIT
ON CHRISTENDOM

Having a form of godliness,
but denying the power thereof.
2 TIMOTHY 3:5

Thou hast a name that thou livest,
and art dead.
REVELATION 3:1

There are five hundred millions of nominal Christians. The state of the majority is unspeakably awful. Formality, worldliness, ungodliness, rejection of Christ's service, ignorance, and indifference—to what an extent does all this prevail. We pray for the heathen—oh! do let us pray for those bearing Christ's name, many in worse than heathen darkness.

Does not one feel as if one ought to begin to give up his life and to cry day and night to God for souls? In answer to prayer, God gives the power of the Holy Ghost.

SPECIAL PETITIONS

_____

_____

_____

_____

_____

HOW TO PRAY:
IN DEEP STILLNESS OF SOUL

My soul waiteth upon God:
from him cometh my salvation.
PSALM 62:1

Prayer has its power in God alone. The nearer a man comes to God Himself, the deeper he enters into God's will; the more he takes hold of God, the more power in prayer.

God must reveal Himself. If it please Him to make Himself known, He can make the heart conscious of His presence. Our posture must be that of holy reverence, of quiet waiting and adoration.

As your month of intercession passes on, and you feel the greatness of your work, be still before God. Thus you will get power to pray.

SPECIAL PETITIONS

_____

_____

_____

_____

_____

Day Twenty

WHAT TO PRAY:
For God's Spirit on the Heathen

Behold, these shall come from far. . .
and these from the land of Sinim.
ISAIAH 49:12

Princes shall come out of Egypt;
Ethiopia shall soon stretch out her hands unto God.
PSALM 68:31

I the LORD will hasten it in his time.
ISAIAH 60:22

Pray for the heathen who are yet without the word. Think of China with her three hundred millions—a million a month dying without Christ. Think of dark Africa with its two hundred millions. Think of thirty millions a year going down into the thick darkness. If Christ gave His life for them, will you not do so? You can give yourself up to intercede for them. Just begin if you have never yet begun, with this simple monthly school of intercession. The ten minutes you give will make you feel this is not enough. God's Spirit will draw you on. Persevere, however feeble you are. Ask God to give you some country or tribe to pray for. Can anything be nobler than to do as Christ did? Give your life for the heathen.

Special Petitions

_____

_____

_____

_____

_____

HOW TO PRAY:
WITH CONFIDENT EXPECTATION
OF AN ANSWER

Call unto me, and I will answer thee,
and shew thee great and mighty things,
which thou knowest not.
JEREMIAH 33:3

Thus saith the LORD God;
I will yet for this be enquired of. . .to do it.
EZEKIEL 36:37

B oth texts refer to promises definitely made, but their fulfillment would depend upon prayer: God would be inquired of to do it.

Pray for God's fulfillment of His promises to His Son and His church, and expect the answer. Plead for the heathen: Plead God's promises.

SPECIAL PETITIONS

_____

_____

_____

_____

Day Twenty-One

WHAT TO PRAY:
For God's Spirit on the Jews

*I will pour upon the house of David,
and upon the inhabitants of Jerusalem,
the spirit of grace and of supplications:
and they shall look unto me
whom they have pierced.*
ZECHARIAH 12:10

*Brethren, my heart's desire
and my prayer to God for Israel is,
that they might be saved.*
ROMANS 10:1

Pray for the Jews. Their return to the God of their fathers stands connected, in a way we cannot tell, with wonderful blessing to the church and with the coming of our Lord Jesus. Let us not think that God has foreordained all this and that we cannot hasten it. In a divine and mysterious way, God has connected His fulfillment of His promise with our prayer. His Spirit's intercession in us is God's forerunner of blessing. Pray for Israel and the work done among them. And pray, too: Amen. Even so, come, Lord Jesus!

Special Petitions

_____

_____

_____

_____

_____

HOW TO PRAY:
WITH THE INTERCESSION
OF THE HOLY SPIRIT

We know not what we should pray for as we ought:
but the Spirit itself maketh intercession
for us with groanings which cannot be uttered.
ROMANS 8:26

I n your ignorance and feebleness believe in the secret indwelling and intercession of the Holy Spirit within you. Yield yourself to His life and leading habitually. He will help your infirmities in prayer. Plead the promises of God even where you do not see how they are to be fulfilled. God knows the mind of the Spirit, because He maketh intercession for the saints according to the will of God. Pray with the simplicity of a little child; pray with the holy awe and reverence of one in whom God's Spirit dwells and prays.

SPECIAL PETITIONS

_____

_____

_____

_____

_____

Day Twenty-Two

WHAT TO PRAY:
For All Who Are in Suffering

Remember them that are in bonds,
as bound with them;
and them which suffer adversity,
as being yourselves also in the body.
HEBREWS 13:3

What a world of suffering we live in! How Jesus sacrificed all and identified Himself with it! Let us in our measure do so, too. The persecuted Stundists and Armenians and Jews, the famine-stricken millions of India, the hidden slavery of Africa, the poverty and wretchedness of our great cities—and so much more: what suffering among those who know God and who know Him not. And then in smaller circles, in ten thousand homes and hearts, what sorrow. In our own neighborhood, how many needing help or comfort. Let us have a heart for, let us think of, the suffering. It will stir us to pray, to work, to hope, to love more. And in a way and time we know not, God will hear our prayer.

Special Petitions

_____

_____

_____

_____

_____

HOW TO PRAY:
Praying Always, and Not Fainting

He spake a parable unto them to this end,
that men ought always to pray,
and not to faint.
Luke 18:1

D o you not begin to feel prayer is really the help for this sinful world? What a need there is of unceasing prayer! The very greatness of the task makes us despair! What can our ten minutes of intercession avail! It is right we feel this: This is the way in which God is calling and preparing us to give our life to prayer. Give yourself wholly to God for men, and amid all your work your heart will be drawn out to men in love, and drawn up to God in dependence and expectation. To a heart thus led by the Holy Spirit, it is possible to pray always and not to faint.

Special Petitions

_____

_____

_____

_____

_____

Day Twenty-Three

WHAT TO PRAY:
For the Holy Spirit in Your Own Work

I also labour, striving according to his working,
which worketh in me mightily.
COLOSSIANS 1:29

You have your own special work; make it a work of intercession. Paul labored, striving according to the working of God in him. Remember, God is not only the Creator, but the great workman, who worketh all in all. You can only do your work in His strength, by Him working in you through the Spirit. Intercede much for those among whom you work, 'til God gives you life for them.

Let us all intercede, too, for each other, for every worker throughout God's church, however solitary or unknown.

Special Petitions

_____

_____

_____

_____

_____

HOW TO PRAY:
IN GOD'S VERY PRESENCE

Draw nigh to God, and he will draw nigh to you.
JAMES 4:8

The nearness of God gives rest and power in prayer. The nearness of God is given to him who makes it his first object. "Draw nigh to God"; seek the nearness to Him, and He will give it; "He will draw nigh to you." Then it becomes easy to pray in faith.

Remember that when first God takes you into the school of intercession it is almost more for your own sake than that of others. You have to be trained to love and wait and pray and believe. Only persevere. Learn to set yourself in His presence, to wait quietly for the assurance that He draws nigh. Enter His holy presence, tarry there, and spread your work before Him. Intercede for the souls you are working among. Get a blessing from God, His Spirit into your own heart, for them.

SPECIAL PETITIONS

_____

_____

_____

_____

_____

Day Twenty-Four

WHAT TO PRAY:
For the Spirit on Your Own Congregation

Beginning at Jerusalem.
Luke 24:47

Each one of us is connected with some congregation or circle of believers, who are to us the part of Christ's body with which we come into most direct contact. They have a special claim on our intercession. Let it be a settled matter between God and you that you are to labor in prayer on its behalf. Pray for the minister and all leaders or workers in the church. Pray for the believers according to their needs. Pray for conversions. Pray for the power of the Spirit to manifest itself. Band yourself with others to join in secret in definite petitions. Let intercession be a definite work, carried on as systematically as preaching or Sunday school. And pray, expecting an answer.

Special Petitions

_____

_____

_____

_____

_____

HOW TO PRAY:
CONTINUALLY

Watchmen. . .which shall never hold
their peace day nor night.
ISAIAH 62:6

His own elect,
which cry day and night unto him.
LUKE 18:7

Night and day praying
exceedingly that we might. . .
perfect that which is lacking in your faith.
1 THESSALONIANS 3:10

A widow indeed. . .trusteth in God,
and continueth in supplications
and prayers night and day.
1 TIMOTHY 5:5

When the glory of God and the love of Christ and the need of souls are revealed to us, the fire of this unceasing intercession will begin to burn in us for those who are near and those who are far off.

SPECIAL PETITIONS

_____

_____

_____

_____

_____

Day Twenty-Five

WHAT TO PRAY:
For More Conversions

He is able also to save them to the uttermost. . .
seeing he ever liveth to make intercession.
HEBREWS 7:25

We will give ourselves continually to prayer,
and to the ministry of the word. . . .
And the word of God increased;
and the number of the disciples
multiplied. . .greatly.
ACTS 6:4, 7

Christ's power to save, and save completely, depends on His unceasing intercession. The apostles withdrawing themselves from other work to give themselves continually to prayer was followed by the number of the disciples multiplying exceedingly. As we, in one day, give ourselves to intercession, we shall have more and mightier conversions. Let us plead for this. Christ is exalted to give repentance. The church exists with the divine purpose and promise of having conversions. Let us not be ashamed to confess our sin and feebleness, and cry to God for more conversions in Christian and heathen lands, of those, too, whom you know and love. Plead for the salvation of sinners.

Special Petitions

_____

_____

_____

_____

_____

HOW TO PRAY:
IN DEEP HUMILITY

> *Truth, Lord: yet the dogs eat of the crumbs. . . .*
> *O woman, great is thy faith:*
> *be it unto thee even as thou wilt.*
> MATTHEW 15:27–28

You feel unworthy and unable to pray aright. To accept this heartily, and to be content still to come and be blessed in your unworthiness, is true humility. It proves its integrity by not seeking for anything, but simply trusting His grace. And so it is the very strength of a great faith that gets a full answer. "Yet the dogs"—let that be your plea as you persevere for someone possibly possessed of the devil. Let not your littleness hinder you for a moment.

SPECIAL PETITIONS

_____

_____

_____

_____

_____

Day Twenty-Six

WHAT TO PRAY:
For the Holy Spirit on Young Converts

Peter and John. . .prayed for them,
that they might receive the Holy Ghost:
(for as yet he was fallen upon none of them:
only they were baptized in the name of the Lord Jesus.)
Acts 8:14–16

Now he which stablisheth us with you in Christ,
and hath anointed us, is God;
who hath also. . .given [us] the earnest
of the Spirit in our hearts.
2 Corinthians 1:21–22

How many new converts who remain feeble; how many who fall into sin; how many who backslide entirely. If we pray for the church, its growth in holiness and devotion to God's service, pray specially for the young converts. How many stand alone, surrounded by temptation; how many have no teaching on the Spirit in them and the power of God to establish them; how many in heathen lands, surrounded by Satan's power. If you pray for the power of the Spirit in the church, pray specially that every young convert may know that he may claim and receive the fullness of the Spirit.

Special Petitions

_____

_____

_____

_____

_____

HOW TO PRAY:
WITHOUT CEASING

> *As for me,*
> *God forbid that I should sin*
> *against the LORD in ceasing*
> *to pray for you.*
> 1 SAMUEL 12:23

It is sin against the Lord to cease praying for others. When once we begin to see how absolutely indispensable intercession is, just as much a duty as loving God or believing in Christ, and how we are called and bound to it as believers, we shall feel that to cease intercession is grievous sin. Let us ask for grace to take up our place as priests with joy, and give our life to bring down the blessing of heaven.

SPECIAL PETITIONS

_____

_____

_____

_____

_____

Day Twenty-Seven

WHAT TO PRAY:
That God's People May Realize Their Calling

I will bless thee. . .and thou shalt be a blessing. . .
in thee shall all families
of the earth be blessed.
GENESIS 12:2–3

God be merciful unto us, and bless us;
and cause his face to shine upon us. . .
that thy way may be known upon earth,
thy saving health among all nations.
PSALM 67:1–2

Abraham was only blessed that he might be a blessing to all the earth. Israel prays for blessing, that God may be known among all nations. Every believer, just as much as Abraham, is only blessed that he may carry God's blessing to the world.

Cry to God that His people may know this, that every believer is only to live for the interests of God and His kingdom. If this truth were preached and believed and practiced, what a revolution it would bring in our mission work. What a host of willing intercessors we should have. Plead with God to work it by the Holy Spirit.

Special Petitions

_____

_____

_____

_____

_____

HOW TO PRAY:
As One Who Has Accepted for Himself
What He Asks for Others

> *Peter said. . .Such as I have give I thee. . . .*
> *The Holy Ghost fell on them,*
> *as on us at the beginning. . . .*
> *God gave them the like gift*
> *as he did unto us.*
> Acts 3:6; 11:15, 17

As you pray for this great blessing on God's people, the Holy Spirit taking entire possession of them for God's service, yield yourself to God and claim the gift anew in faith. Let each thought of feebleness or shortcoming only make you the more urgent in prayer for others; as the blessing comes to them, you, too, will be helped. With every prayer for conversions or mission work, pray that God's people may know how wholly they belong to Him.

Special Petitions

_____

_____

_____

_____

_____

Day Twenty-Eight

WHAT TO PRAY:
That All God's People May Know the Holy Spirit

The Spirit of truth; whom the world. . .
neither knoweth. . .but ye know him;
for he dwelleth with you,
and shall be in you.
John 14:17

Know ye not that your body
is the temple of the Holy Ghost?
1 Corinthians 6:19

The Holy Spirit is the power of God for the salvation of men. He only works as He dwells in the church. He is given to enable believers to live wholly as God would have them live, in the full experience and witness of Him who saves completely. Pray God that every one of His people may know the Holy Spirit! That He in all His fullness is given to them! That they cannot expect to live as their Father would have, without having Him in His fullness, without being filled with Him! Pray that all God's people, even away in churches gathered out of heathendom, may learn to say: I believe in the Holy Ghost.

Special Petitions

_____

_____

_____

_____

_____

HOW TO PRAY:
LABORING FERVENTLY IN PRAYER

Epaphras, who is one of you,
a servant of Christ, saluteth you,
always labouring fervently for you in prayers,
that ye may stand perfect
and complete in all the will of God.
COLOSSIANS 4:12

To a healthy man labor is a delight; in what interests him he labors fervently. The believer who is in full health, whose heart is filled with God's Spirit, labors fervently in prayer. For what? That his brethren may stand perfect and complete in all the will of God; that they may know what God wills for them, how He calls them to live, and be led and walk by the Holy Ghost. Labor fervently in prayer that all God's children may know this, as possible, as divinely sure.

SPECIAL PETITIONS

_____

_____

_____

_____

_____

Day Twenty-Nine

WHAT TO PRAY:
For the Spirit of Intercession

I have chosen you, and ordained you,
that ye should go and bring forth fruit. . .
that whatsoever ye shall ask of the Father
in my name, he may give it you.
John 15:16

Hitherto have ye asked nothing in my name. . . .
At that day ye shall ask in my name.
John 16:24, 26

Has not our school of intercession taught us how little we have prayed in the name of Jesus? He promised His disciples: In that day, when the Holy Spirit comes upon you, ye shall ask in My name. Are there not tens of thousands with us mourning the lack of the power of intercession? Let our intercession today be for them and all God's children, that Christ may teach us that the Holy Spirit is in us; and what it is to live in His fullness, and to yield ourselves to His intercession work within us. The church and the world need nothing so much as a mighty Spirit of intercession to bring down the power of God on earth. Pray for the descent from heaven of the Spirit of intercession for a great prayer revival.

Special Petitions

_____

_____

_____

_____

_____

HOW TO PRAY:
ABIDING IN CHRIST

*If ye abide in me,
and my words abide in you,
ye shall ask what ye will,
and it shall be done unto you.*
JOHN 15:7

Our acceptance with God, our access to Him, is all in Christ. As we consciously abide in Him we have the liberty, not a liberty to our old nature or our self-will, but the divine liberty from all self-will, to ask what we will, in the power of the new nature, and it shall be done. Let us keep this place, and believe even now that our intercession is heard, and that the Spirit of supplication will be given all around us.

SPECIAL PETITIONS

_____

_____

_____

_____

_____

Day Thirty

WHAT TO PRAY:
For the Holy Spirit with the Word of God

*Our gospel came not unto you in word only,
but also in power, and in the Holy Ghost,
and in much assurance.*
1 Thessalonians 1:5

*[Those who] preached the gospel
unto you with the Holy Ghost
sent down from heaven.*
1 Peter 1:12

What numbers of Bibles are being circulated. What numbers of sermons on the Bible are being preached. What numbers of Bibles are being read in home and school. How little blessing when it comes "in word" only; what divine blessing and power when it comes "in the Holy Ghost," when it is preached "with the Holy Ghost sent forth from heaven." Pray for Bible circulation, and preaching and teaching and reading, that it may all be in the Holy Ghost, with much prayer. Pray for the power of the Spirit with the Word in your own neighborhood, wherever it is being read or heard. Let every mention of "The Word of God" waken intercession.

Special Petitions

_____

_____

_____

_____

_____

HOW TO PRAY:
WATCHING AND PRAYING

> *Continue in prayer,*
> *and watch in the same with thanksgiving;*
> *withal praying also for us,*
> *that God would open unto us*
> *a door of utterance.*
> COLOSSIANS 4:2–3

Do you not see how all depends upon God and prayer? As long as He lives and loves and hears and works, as long as there are souls with hearts closed to the Word, as long as there is work to be done in carrying the Word—pray without ceasing. Continue steadfastly in prayer, watching therein with thanksgiving. These words are for every Christian.

SPECIAL PETITIONS

_____

_____

_____

_____

_____

Day Thirty-One

WHAT TO PRAY:
For the Spirit of Christ in His People

I am the vine, ye are the branches.
John 15:5

That ye should do as I have done to you.
John 13:15

As branches we are to be so like the vine, so entirely identified with it, that all may see that we have the same nature and life and spirit. When we pray for the Spirit, let us not only think of a Spirit of power, but the very disposition and temper of Christ Jesus. Ask and expect nothing less: For yourself and all God's children, cry for it.

Special Petitions

_____

_____

_____

_____

_____

HOW TO PRAY:
STRIVING IN PRAYER

> *That ye strive together with me*
> *in your prayers to God for me.*
> ROMANS 15:30

> *I would that ye knew*
> *what great conflict I have for you.*
> COLOSSIANS 2:1

All the powers of evil seek to hinder us in prayer. Prayer is conflict with opposing forces. It needs the whole heart and all our strength. May God give us grace to strive in prayer 'til we prevail.

SPECIAL PETITIONS

_____

_____

_____

_____

_____

PRAYER
VITALS

Facts and Figures, Goals and Guidance

Tracy M. Sumner

Contents

Introduction

Someone once said that praying is as natural to a human as breathing. And yet so few of us really know how to do it—at least in the way that God says to do it. In fact, the people who were the closest to Jesus—His twelve disciples—didn't have a clue how they should pray. That's why they asked Him one day, "Lord, teach us to pray!"

That's what this book is all about.

This book is a basically a collection of lists—some of them straight out of the Bible and some of them from other sources. Each of these lists has to do with prayer, either how to pray or how others have prayed in the past.

But this book isn't meant to be just a fun collection of information—even though we hope you enjoy reading it. It's meant to challenge you and to get you thinking about what it really means to pray. There isn't a lot of commentary on the scriptures, facts, or quotations we've included—we'll leave the interpretations and applications up to you.

1
What's in The *Book*?
Some Biblical What's, How's, and Where's on Prayer

Since the real message behind the stories, promises, and commands in the Bible is relating to God in a personal way, it only makes sense that His written Word would have a lot to say about prayer.

That it most certainly does!

This chapter is a collection of biblical advice, commands, promises, and wisdom on the subject of prayer. And while we couldn't get everything the Bible has to say about prayer to fit in this chapter, what you're about to read will give you some pretty solid guidelines for your life of prayer.

Some Biblical Prayer Trivia

- **The Bible's first mention of prayer:** "And to Seth, to him also there was born a son; and he called his name Enos: then began men to call upon the name of the Lord" (Genesis 4:26).
- **The Bible's first use of the word pray (in reference to speaking to God):** "My Lord, if now I have found favour in thy sight, pass not away, I pray thee, from thy servant" (Genesis 18:3).
- **The Bible's first use of the word prayer:** "For thou, O Lord of hosts, God of Israel, hast revealed to thy servant, saying, I will build thee an house: therefore hath thy servant found in his heart to pray this prayer unto thee" (2 Samuel 7:27).
- **The Bible's last use of the word prayer:** "And the smoke of the incense, which came with the prayers of the saints, ascended up before God out of the angel's hand" (Revelation 8:4).
- **Number of verses that include the word prayer: 128**
- **Number of prayers in the Bible: approximately 650**
- **Number of answered prayers in the Bible: approximately 450**

Physical Postures for Prayer in the Bible

- **Bowing heads:** "And the people believed: and when they heard that the Lord had visited the children of Israel, and that he had looked upon their affliction, then they bowed their heads and worshipped" (Exodus 4:31).
- **Standing:** "And Solomon stood before the altar of the Lord in the presence of all the congregation of Israel, and spread forth his hands toward heaven" (1 Kings 8:22).
- **Kneeling:** "And it was so, that when Solomon had made an end

of praying all this prayer and supplication unto the LORD, he arose from before the altar of the LORD, from kneeling on his knees with his hands spread up to heaven" (1 Kings 8:54).

- **On their faces before God:** "And Jehoshaphat bowed his head with his face to the ground: and all Judah and the inhabitants of Jerusalem fell before the LORD, worshipping the LORD" (2 Chronicles 20:18; see also Matthew 26:39).

PRAYER: ALSO KNOWN (IN THE BIBLE) AS. . .

1. **Bowing the knees:** "For this cause I bow my knees unto the Father of our Lord Jesus Christ" (Ephesians 3:14).

2. **Looking up:** "My voice shalt thou hear in the morning, O LORD; in the morning will I direct my prayer unto thee, and will look up" (Psalm 5:3).

3. **Lifting up the soul:** "Unto thee, O LORD, do I lift up my soul" (Psalm 25:1).

4. **Lifting up the heart:** "Let us lift up our heart with our hands unto God in the heavens" (Lamentations 3:41).

5. **Pouring out the heart:** "Trust in him at all times; ye people, pour out your heart before him: God is a refuge for us" (Psalm 62:8).

6. **Pouring out the soul:** "And Hannah answered and said, No, my lord, I am a woman of a sorrowful spirit: I have drunk neither wine nor strong drink, but have poured out my soul before the LORD" (1 Samuel 1:15).

7. **Calling upon the name of the Lord:** "And he removed from thence unto a mountain on the east of Bethel, and pitched his tent, having Bethel on the west, and Hai on the east: and there he builded an altar unto the LORD, and called upon the name of the LORD" (Genesis 12:8; see also Psalm 116:4; Acts 22:16).

8. **Crying unto God:** "Hear, O LORD, when I cry with my voice: have mercy also upon me, and answer me" (Psalm 27:7; see also Psalm 34:6).

9. **Drawing near to God:** "But it is good for me to draw near to God: I have put my trust in the Lord GOD, that I may declare all thy works" (Psalm 73:28; see also Hebrews 10:22).

10. **Crying to heaven:** "And for this cause Hezekiah the king, and the prophet Isaiah the son of Amoz, prayed and cried to heaven" (2 Chronicles 32:20).

11. **Beseeching (pleading with) the Lord:** "And Moses besought the LORD his God, and said, LORD, why doth thy wrath wax hot against thy people, which thou hast brought forth out of the land of Egypt

with great power, and with a mighty hand?" (Exodus 32:11).

12. **Seeking unto God:** "If thou wouldest seek unto God betimes, and make thy supplication to the Almighty" (Job 8:5).

13. **Seeking the face of the Lord:** "When thou saidst, Seek ye my face; my heart said unto thee, Thy face, LORD, will I seek" (Psalm 27:8).

14. **Making supplication:** "If thou wouldest seek unto God betimes, and make thy supplication to the Almighty" (Job 8:5; see also Jeremiah 36:7).

25 BIBLICAL PRAYER HOW-TO'S: WE SHOULD PRAY. . .

1. **In the Holy Spirit:** "Praying always with all prayer and supplication in the Spirit, and watching thereunto with all perseverance and supplication for all saints" (Ephesians 6:18; see also Jude 1:20).

2. **In faith:** "And all things, whatsoever ye shall ask in prayer, believing, ye shall receive" (Matthew 21:22; see also James 1:6).

3. **With full assurance:** "Let us draw near with a true heart in full assurance of faith, having our hearts sprinkled from an evil conscience, and our bodies washed with pure water" (Hebrews 10:22).

4. **With a heart of forgiveness for others who have hurt us:** "And forgive us our debts, as we forgive our debtors" (Matthew 6:12).

5. **With all the heart:** "And ye shall seek me, and find me, when ye shall search for me with all your heart" (Jeremiah 29:13; see also Lamentations 3:41; Psalm 119:58).

6. **With a prepared heart:** "If thou prepare thine heart, and stretch out thine hands toward him. . ." (Job 11:13).

7. **With a true heart:** "Let us draw near with a true heart in full assurance of faith, having our hearts sprinkled from an evil conscience, and our bodies washed with pure water" (Hebrews 10:22).

8. **With a poured out soul:** "When I remember these things, I pour out my soul in me: for I had gone with the multitude, I went with them to the house of God, with the voice of joy and praise, with a multitude that kept holyday" (Psalm 42:4).

9. **In the spirit and in truth;** "Ye worship ye know not what: we know what we worship: for salvation is of the Jews. But the hour cometh, and now is, when the true worshippers shall worship the Father in spirit and in truth: for the Father seeketh such to worship him. God is a Spirit: and they that worship him must worship him in spirit and in truth" (John 4:22–24; see also 1 Corinthians 14:15).

10. **With full confidence in God:** "When I cry unto thee, then shall mine enemies turn back: this I know; for God is for me" (Psalm 56:9; see also Psalm 86:7).

11. **With full confidence we are heard:** "And this is the confidence that we have in him, that, if we ask any thing according to his will, he heareth us" (1 John 5:14).

12. **With an attitude of submission to God:** "Father, if thou be willing, remove this cup from me: nevertheless not my will, but thine, be done" (Luke 22:42).

13. **Without use of deceitful lips:** "Hear the right, O Lord, attend unto my cry, give ear unto my prayer, that goeth not out of feigned lips" (Psalm 17:1).

14. **Thoughtfully:** "Be not rash with thy mouth, and let not thine heart be hasty to utter any thing before God: for God is in heaven, and thou upon earth: therefore let thy words be few" (Ecclesiastes 5:2).

15. **With holiness:** "I will therefore that men pray every where, lifting up holy hands, without wrath and doubting" (1 Timothy 2:8).

16. **With humility:** "If my people, which are called by my name, shall humble themselves, and pray, and seek my face, and turn from their wicked ways; then will I hear from heaven, and will forgive their sin, and will heal their land" (2 Chronicles 7:14; see also 33:12).

17. **With truth:** "The Lord is nigh unto all them that call upon him, to all that call upon him in truth" (Psalm 145:18; see also John 4:24).

18. **With a sincere desire to be heard:** "Let thine ear now be attentive, and thine eyes open, that thou mayest hear the prayer of thy servant, which I pray before thee now, day and night, for the children of Israel thy servants, and confess the sins of the children of Israel, which we have sinned against thee: both I and my father's house have sinned" (Nehemiah 1:6; see also Psalm 17:1; 55:1; 61:1).

19. **With a desire to receive an answer:** "Hear, O Lord, when I cry with my voice: have mercy also upon me, and answer me" (Psalm 27:7; see also Psalm 102:2; 108:6, 143:1).

20. **With boldness:** "Let us therefore come boldly unto the throne of grace, that we may obtain mercy, and find grace to help in time of need" (Hebrews 4:16).

21. **With seriousness:** "Night and day praying exceedingly that we might see your face, and might perfect that which is lacking in your faith?" (1 Thessalonians 3:10; see also James 5:17).

22. **With great persistence:** "And he said, Let me go, for the day breaketh. And he said, I will not let thee go, except thou bless me"

(Genesis 32:26; see also Luke 11:9; 18:1–7).

23. **At all times:** "Now she that is a widow indeed, and desolate, trusteth in God, and continueth in supplications and prayers night and day" (1 Timothy 5:5).

24. **Without ceasing:** "Pray without ceasing" (1 Thessalonians 5:17).

25. **Without worry:** "Be careful for nothing; but in every thing by prayer and supplication with thanksgiving let your requests be made known unto God" (Philippians 4:6).

SOME GOOD THINGS TO BRING WITH YOU WHEN YOU PRAY

1. **Repentance:** "When thy people Israel be smitten down before the enemy, because they have sinned against thee, and shall turn again to thee, and confess thy name, and pray, and make supplication unto thee in this house" (1 Kings 8:33; see also Jeremiah 36:7).

2. **Confession:** "And it came to pass, when I heard these words, that I sat down and wept, and mourned certain days, and fasted, and prayed before the God of heaven" (Nehemiah 1:4; see also Nehemiah 1:7).

3. **Humility:** "And Abraham answered and said, Behold now, I have taken upon me to speak unto the LORD, which am but dust and ashes" (Genesis 18:27).

4. **Weeping:** "They shall come with weeping, and with supplications will I lead them: I will cause them to walk by the rivers of waters in a straight way, wherein they shall not stumble: for I am a father to Israel, and Ephraim is my firstborn" (Jeremiah 31:9; see also Hosea 12:4).

5. **Fasting:** "And it came to pass, when I heard these words, that I sat down and wept, and mourned certain days, and fasted, and prayed before the God of heaven" (Nehemiah 1:4; see also Daniel 9:3; Acts 13:3).

6. **Watchfulness:** "But the end of all things is at hand: be ye therefore sober, and watch unto prayer" (1 Peter 4:7; see also Luke 21:36).

7. **Praise:** "I cried unto him with my mouth, and he was extolled with my tongue" (Psalm 66:17).

8. **Thanksgiving:** "Be careful for nothing; but in every thing by prayer and supplication with thanksgiving let your requests be made known unto God (Philippians 4:6; see also Colossians 4:2).

9. **Persistence:** "I say unto you, Though he will not rise and give him, because he is his friend, yet because of his importunity he will rise and give him as many as he needeth" (Luke 11:8).

12 CONDITIONS FOR ANSWERED PRAYER

1. **Seeking God:** "I sought the LORD, and he heard me, and delivered me from all my fears" (Psalm 34:4).

2. **Seek God with all the heart:** "Then shall ye call upon me, and ye shall go and pray unto me, and I will hearken unto you. And ye shall seek me, and find me, when ye shall search for me with all your heart" (Jeremiah 29:12–13).

3. **Waiting on God:** "I waited patiently for the LORD; and he inclined unto me, and heard my cry" (Psalm 40:1).

4. **Returning to God:** "If my people, which are called by my name, shall humble themselves, and pray, and seek my face, and turn from their wicked ways; then will I hear from heaven, and will forgive their sin, and will heal their land" (2 Chronicles 7:14).

5. **Asking in faith:** "And the prayer of faith shall save the sick, and the Lord shall raise him up; and if he have committed sins, they shall be forgiven him" (James 5:15).

6. **Asking in Christ's name:** "And whatsoever ye shall ask in my name, that will I do, that the Father may be glorified in the Son" (John 14:13).

7. **Asking in agreement with God's will:** "And this is the confidence that we have in him, that, if we ask any thing according to his will, he heareth us" (1 John 5:14).

8. **Fearing God:** "He will fulfil the desire of them that fear him: he also will hear their cry, and will save them" (Psalm 145:19).

9. **Keeping God's Commandments:** "And whatsoever we ask, we receive of him, because we keep his commandments, and do those things that are pleasing in his sight" (1 John 3:22).

10. **Abiding (remaining) in Christ:** "If ye abide in me, and my words abide in you, ye shall ask what ye will, and it shall be done unto you" (John 15:7).

11. **Being humble:** "If my people, which are called by my name, shall humble themselves, and pray, and seek my face, and turn from their wicked ways; then will I hear from heaven, and will forgive their sin, and will heal their land" (2 Chronicles 7:14; see also Psalm 9:12).

12. **Living in righteousness:** "Confess your faults one to another, and pray one for another, that ye may be healed. The effectual fervent prayer of a righteous man availeth much" (James 5:16; see also Psalm 34:15).

22 Great Biblical Promises about Prayer

1. **"If my people, which are called by my name, shall humble themselves, and pray, and seek my face, and turn from their wicked ways;** then will I hear from heaven, and will forgive their sin, and will heal their land" (2 Chronicles 7:14).

2. **"The LORD is nigh unto all them that call upon him, to all that call upon him in truth.** He will fulfil the desire of them that fear him: he also will hear their cry, and will save them" (Psalm 145:18–19).

3. **"The sacrifice of the wicked is an abomination to the LORD:** but the prayer of the upright is his delight" (Proverbs 15:8).

4. **"And it shall come to pass, that before they call, I will answer;** and while they are yet speaking, I will hear" (Isaiah 65:24).

5. **"Call unto me, and I will answer thee,** and show thee great and mighty things, which thou knowest not" (Jeremiah 33:3).

6. **"And all things, whatsoever ye shall ask in prayer,** believing, ye shall receive" (Matthew 21:22).

7. **"Be not ye therefore like unto them:** for your Father knoweth what things ye have need of, before ye ask him" (Matthew 6:8).

8. **"Ask, and it shall be given you;** seek, and ye shall find; knock, and it shall be opened unto you" (Matthew 7:7; Luke 11:9).

9. **"If ye then, being evil, know how to give good gifts unto your children,** how much more shall your Father which is in heaven give good things to them that ask him?" (Matthew 7:11; see also Luke 11:13).

10. **"Again I say unto you,** That if two of you shall agree on earth as touching any thing that they shall ask, it shall be done for them of my Father which is in heaven" (Matthew 18:19).

11. **"Therefore I say unto you,** What things soever ye desire, when ye pray, believe that ye receive them, and ye shall have them" (Mark 11:24).

12. **"But I know,** that even now, whatsoever thou wilt ask of God, God will give it thee" (John 11:22).

13. **"And whatsoever ye shall ask in my name,** that will I do, that the Father may be glorified in the Son" (John 14:13).

14. **"If ye shall ask any thing in my name,** I will do it" (John 14:14).

15. **"If ye abide in me,** and my words abide in you, ye shall ask what ye will, and it shall be done unto you" (John 15:7).

16. **"Ye have not chosen me,** but I have chosen you, and ordained you, that ye should go and bring forth fruit, and that your fruit should remain: that whatsoever ye shall ask of the Father in my

name, he may give it you" (John 15:16).

17. **"And in that day ye shall ask me nothing.** Verily, verily, I say unto you, Whatsoever ye shall ask the Father in my name, he will give it you" (John 16:23).

18. **"Hitherto have ye asked nothing in my name:** ask, and ye shall receive, that your joy may be full" (John 16:24).

19. **"Likewise the Spirit also helpeth our infirmities:** for we know not what we should pray for as we ought: but the Spirit itself maketh intercession for us with groanings which cannot be uttered" (Romans 8:26).

20. **"For the eyes of the Lord are over the righteous,** and his ears are open unto their prayers" (1 Peter 3:12).

21. **"And this is the confidence that we have in him,** that, if we ask any thing according to his will, he heareth us" (1 John 5:14).

22. **"And if we know that he hear us, whatsoever we ask,** we know that we have the petitions that we desired of him" (1 John 5:15).

PRAYER—IN PRIVATE AND IN PUBLIC

The Bible clearly teaches that God's people should get alone with God in a private place to pray (see Matthew 6:6, for example). Yet the same Bible extols the virtues of public prayer among God's people. Here are biblical examples of both:

20 BIBLICAL EXAMPLES OF PRIVATE PRAYER

1. **Jesus** (Matthew 14:23; 26:36; 26:39)
2. **Lot** (Genesis 19:20)
3. **Abraham's servant** (Genesis 24:9–12)
4. **Jacob** (Genesis 32:9–12)
5. **Gideon** (Judges 6:22, 36, 39)
6. **Hannah** (1 Samuel 1:9–10)
7. **David** (2 Samuel 7:18–29)
8. **Hezekiah** (2 Kings 20:1–3)
9. **Isaiah** (2 Kings 20:11)
10. **Manasseh** (2 Chronicles 33:18–19)
11. **Ezra** (Ezra 9:5–6)
12. **Nehemiah** (Nehemiah 2:4)
13. **Jeremiah** (Jeremiah 32:16–25)
14. **Daniel** (Daniel 9:3, 17)
15. **Jonah** (Jonah 2:1)
16. **Habakkuk** (Habakkuk 1:2)
17. **Anna** (Luke 2:36–37)
18. **Saul** (Acts 9:11)

19. **Peter** (Acts 9:40; 10:9)
20. **Cornelius** (Acts 10:30)

BIBLICAL EXAMPLES OF PUBLIC PRAYER

1. **Joshua** (Joshua 7:6–9)
2. **David** (1 Chronicles 29:10–19)
3. **Solomon** (2 Chronicles 6)
4. **Jehoshaphat** (2 Chronicles 20:5–13)
5. **The Levites** (Nehemiah 9)
6. **The Jews of Jesus' time** (Luke 1:10)
7. **First-generation Christians** (Acts 2:46; 4:24; 12:5; 12:12)
8. **Peter and John** (Acts 3:1)
9. **Teachers and prophets at Antioch** (Acts 13:1–3)
10. **The apostle Paul** (Acts 16:16)

30 IMPORTANT PRAYERS (SEE TEXT OF FIRST 20 IN CHAPTER 5)

1. **Abraham's bargaining for Sodom** (Genesis 18:16–33)
2. **Jacob's prayer for Esau's mercy** (Genesis 32:6–12)
3. **Jacob's prayer for blessing at Peniel** (Genesis 32:24–30)
4. **Moses' prayer at the burning bush** (Exodus 3:1–4:18)
5. **Moses' confession for Israel in the wilderness** (Exodus 32:9–14)
6. **Moses' plea for God's presence** (Exodus 33:12–34:9)
7. **Joshua's prayer after defeat at Ai** (Joshua 7:6–15)
8. **Hannah's prayer for a child** (1 Samuel 1:9–11)
9. **David's prayer when he was denied the privilege of building the temple** (2 Samuel 7:18–29)
10. **Solomon's request for wisdom** (1 Kings 3:4–10)
11. **Solomon's temple dedication prayer** (1 Kings 8:22–61)
12. **Hezekiah's petitions for Judah's deliverance** (2 Kings 19:14–19)
13. **Hezekiah's plea for his life** (2 Kings 20:1–3)
14. **Ezra's confession of his people's sins** (Ezra 9:5–15)
15. **Nehemiah's prayer for success** (Nehemiah 1:1–11)
16. **Job's contrite prayer** (Job 42:1–6)
17. **David's prayer for pardon and confession of sin** (Psalm 51)
18. **David's prayer for deliverance from evil men** (Psalm 140)
19. **Isaiah's prayer for mercy** (Isaiah 64:1–12)
20. **Daniel's confession on behalf of his people** (Daniel 9:1–19)
21. **Jonah's contrite prayer** (Jonah 2:1–9)
22. **Habakkuk's questioning prayer** (Habakkuk 1:1–2:1)
23. **Habakkuk's prayer of praise** (Habakkuk 3:1–19)
24. **Jesus' "High Priestly" prayer** (John 17)

25.   **Jesus' prayer at Gethsemane** (Matthew 26:36–42)
26.   **Jesus' prayer for His enemies** (Luke 23:33–34)
27.   **The prayer of the dying, penitent criminal** (Luke 23:40–42)
28.   **The church's prayer for boldness** (Acts 4:19, 23–31)
29.   **Stephen, as he was martyred** (Acts 7:59–60)
30.   **Paul, for the Ephesians** (Ephesians 1:1, 15–23; 3:14–21)

55 BIBLICAL EXAMPLES OF ANSWERED PRAYER

1.   **Cain, for protection from God** (Genesis 4:13–15)
2.   **Abraham, for a son** (Genesis 15)
3.   **Abraham, for Sodom** (Genesis 18:23–33)
4.   **Abraham, for Ishmael** (Genesis 17:18–20)
5.   **Abraham, for Abimelech** (Genesis 20:9, 17)
6.   **Hagar, for deliverance** (Genesis 16:7–13)
7.   **Abraham's servant, for guidance** (Genesis 24:12–52)
8.   **Rebecca, concerning her pains in pregnancy** (Genesis 25:21–26)
9.   **Jacob, for protection from Esau** (Genesis 32:9–32; 33:1–17)
10.   **Moses, at the Red Sea** (Exodus 14:15–16)
11.   **Moses, at the waters of Marah** (Exodus 15:22–25)
12.   **Moses, at Mount Horeb** (Exodus 17:4–6)
13.   **Moses, in battle with the Amalekites** (Exodus 17:8–14)
14.   **Moses, when Israelites complained for meat** (Numbers 11:11–34)
15.   **Moses, for Miriam's leprosy** (Numbers 12:10, 13–15)
16.   **Moses, Aaron, and Samuel** (Psalm 99:6)
17.   **The people of Israel, for freedom from bondage** (Exodus 2:23–25; 3:7–10; Acts 7:34)
18.   **The people of Israel, for protection from Pharaoh's army** (Exodus 14:10–30)
19.   **The people of Israel, for protection from the king of Mesopotamia** (Judges 3:8–9, 15)
20.   **Ammon** (Judges 10:6–18; 11:1–33)
21.   **The people of Israel for freedom from Babylonian bondage** (Nehemiah 9:1, 5, 27)
22.   **Gideon, asking for a sign from God** (Judges 6:36–40)
23.   **Manoah, asking about Samson** (Judges 13:8–9)
24.   **Samson, asking for strength** (Judges 16:28–30)
25.   **Hannah, asking to become a mother** (1 Samuel 1:9–20)
26.   **David, asking whether Keilah would be delivered into his hands** (1 Samuel 23:10–12)
27.   **David, asking about Ziklag** (1 Samuel 30:1–8)
28.   **David, asking whether he should go into Judah after Saul's**

death (2 Samuel 2:1)

29. **David, asking whether he should go to war against the Philistines** (2 Samuel 5:19–25)

30. **Solomon, asking for wisdom** (1 Kings 3:5–13)

31. **Elijah, when raising the widow's son from the dead** (1 Kings 17:10, 21–22)

32. **Elijah, asking for a sign from God regarding his sacrifice** (1 Kings 18:36–38)

33. **Elijah, asking for rain** (1 Kings 17:1; 18:1, 42–45)

34. **Elisha, leading against the Syrian army** (2 Kings 6:17–20)

35. **Jabez, asking for prosperity** (1 Chronicles 4:10)

36. **Abijah, for victory over Jeroboam** (2 Chronicles 13:3–18)

37. **Asa, for victory over Zerah** (2 Chronicles 14:8–15)

38. **The people of Judah** (2 Chronicles 15:15)

39. **Jehoshaphat, for victory over the Canaanites** (2 Chronicles 18:31; 20:6–27)

40. **Jehoahaz, for victory over Hazael** (2 Kings 13:4)

41. **Hezekiah and Isaiah, for deliverance from Sennacherib** (2 Kings 19:14–20; 2 Chronicles 32:20–22)

42. **To save Hezekiah's life** (2 Kings 20:1–7)

43. **The Reubenites, for deliverance from the Hagarites** (1 Chronicles 5:18–20)

44. **Manasseh, for deliverance from the king of Babylon** (2 Chronicles 33:11–13)

45. **The Jews, returning from the captivity** (Ezra 8:21, 23)

46. **Ezekiel, to have the baking of his bread of affliction changed** (Ezekiel 4:12–15)

47. **Daniel, for the interpretation of Nebuchadnezzar's dream** (Daniel 2:1, 16–23)

48. **Daniel, interceding for the people** (Daniel 9:20–27)

49. **Daniel, in a vision** (Daniel 10:9–12)

50. **Zacharias, for a son** (Luke 1:13)

51. **The leper, for healing** (Matthew 8:2–3; Mark 1:40–43; Luke 5:12–13)

52. **The centurion, for his servant** (Matthew 8:5–13; Luke 7:3–10; John 4:50–51)

53. **Peter, asking that Tabitha (Dorcas) be restored to life** (Acts 9:40)

54. **The disciples, for Peter** (Acts 12:5–17)

55. **Paul, to be restored to health** (2 Chronicles 1:9–11)

BIBLICAL EXAMPLES OF PERSISTENT PRAYER

1. **Jacob, for God's blessing** (Genesis 32:24–30)
2. **Moses, for his people** (Exodus 33:12–16)
3. **Elijah, for confirmation of God's calling** (1 Kings 18:22–44)
4. **The two blind men of Jericho for healing** (Matthew 20:30–31; Mark 10:48; Luke 18:39)
5. **The non-Jewish, Syro-Phoenician woman, for her daughter's healing** (Matthew 15:22–28)
6. **The Roman centurion, for his servant's healing** (Matthew 8:5; Luke 7:2–9)

EXAMPLES OF PRAYER WITH FASTING (ABSTAINING FROM FOOD)

1. **Jesus** (Matthew 4:1–2)
2. **Moses** (Exodus 34:27–28; Deuteronomy 9:9, 18)
3. **Elijah** (1 Kings 19:8–9)
4. **The nation of Israel** (Judges 20:26; Ezra 8:21; Esther 4:3)
5. **The Ninevites** (Jonah 3:5–8)
6. **David** (2 Samuel 12:16; Psalm 109:24)
7. **Nehemiah** (Nehemiah 1:1, 4)
8. **Esther** (Esther 4:15–16)
9. **Daniel** (Daniel 9:2–3)
10. **Disciples of John the Baptist** (Matthew 9:14)
11. **Anna** (Luke 2:36–37)
12. **Cornelius** (Acts 10:30)
13. **The early Christians** (Acts 13:1–2)

2
The Biblical Pillars of Prayer
THE FIVE DIFFERENT WAYS GOD WANTS
YOU TO PRAY TO HIM

There are literally hundreds of references to prayer throughout the Bible. But did you know not all prayers are the same? In the Bible, there are five basic types of prayer, all of which are equally important to God: praise/worship, confession/penitence, petition/supplication (also known as requests), thanksgiving, and intercession.

In this chapter, you can read what the Bible has to say about each of these types of prayer.

PILLAR 1: PRAISE/WORSHIP

The Bible is filled with prayers of praise and worship to God—especially in the book of Psalms. Praise and worship are basically how we humans relate to God by verbally giving Him the glory for His greatness, goodness, power, and other attributes that make Him God.

10 BIBLICAL THINGS TO KNOW ABOUT PRAISE/WORSHIP

1. **It is fitting to praise God because He is God** (Psalm 33:1; 147:1).
2. **It should be offered from the soul** (Psalm 103:1; 104:1, 35).
3. **It should be offered with the entire heart** (Psalm 9:1; 111:1; 138:1).
4. **It should be done with an upright heart** (Psalm 119:7).
5. **It should be done with the mouth** (Psalm 51:15; 63:3; 119:171).
6. **It should be done joyfully** (Psalm 63:5; 98:4).
7. **It should be done with gladness** (2 Chronicles 29:30; Jeremiah 33:11).
8. **It should be done with thankfulness** (1 Chronicles 16:4; Psalm 147:7).
9. **It should be done continually** (Psalm 35:28; 71:6).
10. **It should be offered throughout life** (Psalm 104:33).

BIBLICAL REASONS GOD IS WORTHY OF PRAISE/WORSHIP

1. **His majesty** (Psalm 93:1; 96:6)
2. **His glory** (Psalm 138:5; Ezekiel 3:12)
3. **His excellence** (Exodus 15:7; Psalm 148:13)
4. **His greatness** (1 Chronicles 16:25; Psalm 145:3)
5. **His holiness** (Exodus 15:11; Isaiah 6:3)

6. **His wisdom** (Daniel 2:20; Jude 1:25)
7. **His power** (Psalm 21:13)
8. **His goodness** (Psalm 107:8; 118:1; 136:1; Jeremiah 33:11)
9. **His mercy** (2 Chronicles 20:21; Psalm 89:1; 118:1–4; 136)
10. **His lovingkindness and truth** (Psalm 138:2)
11. **His faithfulness and truth** (Isaiah 25:1)
12. **His salvation** (Psalm 18:46; Isaiah 25:9; 61:10; Luke 1:68–69)
13. **His wonderful deeds and work** (Psalm 89:5; 150:2; Isaiah 25:1)
14. **His comfort** (Psalm 23:4; Isaiah 12:1)
15. **His judgment** (Psalm 101:1)
16. **His wise counsel** (Psalm 16:7; Jeremiah 32:19)
17. **His faithfulness in fulfilling His promises** (1 Kings 8:56)
18. **His willingness to pardon of sin** (Psalm 103:1–3; Hosea 14:2)
19. **His deliverance** (Psalm 40:1–3)
20. **His protection** (Psalm 28:7; 59:17)
21. **His answers to prayer** (Psalm 28:6; 118:21)
22. **His spiritual blessings** (Psalm 103:2; Ephesians 1:3)
23. **His temporal blessings** (Psalm 136:1, 25)
24. **His continuous blessings** (Psalm 68:19)

21 BIBLICAL EXAMPLES OF PRAISE AND WORSHIP

1. **Melchizedek** (Genesis 14:18–20)
2. **Moses and the Israelites** (Exodus 15:1–21)
3. **Miriam** (Exodus 15:21)
4. **Jethro** (Exodus 18:10)
5. **The Israelites** (1 Chronicles 16:36)
6. **David** (1 Chronicles 29:10–13; Psalm 119:164)
7. **Deborah** (Judges 5)
8. **Hannah** (1 Samuel 2:1–10)
9. **The priests and Levites** (Ezra 3:10–11)
10. **Ezra** (Nehemiah 8:6)
11. **King Hezekiah** (Isaiah 38:2, 19)
12. **Zacharias** (Luke 1:59, 62–64)
13. **The shepherds** (Luke 2:20)
14. **Simeon** (Luke 2:25, 27–28)
15. **Anna** (Luke 2:36–38)
16. **Multitudes** (Luke 18:43)
17. **Jesus' disciples** (Luke 19:37–38)
18. **The apostles** (Luke 24:50–53)
19. **The first converts** (Acts 2:44, 46–47)
20. **The lame man who was healed** (Acts 3:2, 6–8)
21. **Paul and Silas in prison** (Acts 16:25)

BIBLICAL TERMS FOR THE PRAISE OF GOD

1. **Fruit of the lips** (Hebrews 13:15)
2. **Voice of praise** (Psalm 66:8)
3. **Voice of triumph** (Psalm 47:1)
4. **Voice of melody** (Isaiah 51:3)
5. **Voice of a psalm** (Psalm 98:5)
6. **Garment of praise** (Isaiah 61:3)
7. **Sacrifice of praise** (Hebrews 13:15)
8. **Sacrifices of joy** (Psalm 27:6)
9. **Calves of the lips** (Hosea 14:2)

CONFESSION/PENITENCE

One of God's attributes that is so worthy of our praise and worship is His willingness and desire to forgive our sins. The Bible teaches that in order to receive that forgiveness, we must come to God praying prayers of confession ("Yes, I did it") and penitence ("With Your power, I endeavor to stop doing it").

BIBLICAL THINGS TO KNOW ABOUT CONFESSION/PENITENCE

1. **God requires it** (Leviticus 5:5; Hosea 5:15).
2. **The Bible strongly encourages it** (Joshua 7:19; Jeremiah 3:13; James 5:16).
3. **It is the key to receiving God's mercy and forgiveness** (Proverbs 28:13).
4. **It should include a request for forgiveness** (2 Samuel 24:10; Psalm 25:11; 51:1; Jeremiah 14:7–9, 20)
5. **It should be done in humility** (Isaiah 64:5–6).
6. **There should be sorrow for sin** (Psalm 38:18; Lamentations 1:20).
7. **It should include the abandonment of sin** (Proverbs 28:13).
8. **It may include some restitution** (Numbers 5:6–7).
9. **It should be full and unreserved** (Psalm 32:5; 51:3; 106:6).
10. **It is followed by God's pardon/forgiveness** (Psalm 32:5; 1 John 1:9).

BIBLICAL EXAMPLES OF CONFESSION/PENITENCE

1. **Aaron** (Numbers 12:11)
2. **The Israelites** (Numbers 21:6–7; 1 Samuel 7:6; 12:1, 19)
3. **King Saul** (1 Samuel 15:24)
4. **King David** (2 Samuel 24:10; Psalm 51)
5. **Ezra** (Ezra 9:5–6)
6. **Nehemiah** (Nehemiah 1:6–7)
7. **Levites** (Nehemiah 9:4, 33–34)

8. **Job** (Job 7:20)
9. **Daniel** (Daniel 9:4)
10. **Peter** (Luke 5:8)
11. **The thief on the cross** (Luke 23:39–42)

PETITION/SUPPLICATION (ALSO KNOWN AS REQUESTS)

When we use the term "answered prayer," we are referring to the type of prayer called petitions or supplications—or, in more modern language, requests. This is the part of prayer where we ask God for something. God loves to hear and answer His people's prayers of petition and supplication. That is largely because these prayers demonstrate the kind of dependence that is so fitting a heavenly Father/child of God relationship.

10 BIBLICAL THINGS TO KNOW ABOUT PETITIONS/SUPPLICATIONS

1. **Faith is essential in receiving the answer you seek** (Mark 11:23–24; James 5:15).
2. **Supplications should be offered in accordance with God's known will** (1 John 5:14–15).
3. **Supplications should be offered with right motives** (James 4:3).
4. **We should not worry but instead offer prayers *and* supplications** (Philippians 4:6).
5. **We should wait on God for our answers** (Psalm 40:1).
6. **We should ask in Christ's name** (John 14:13).
7. **We should approach God and ask boldly** (Hebrews 4:16).
8. **Keeping God's commandments is necessary for an answer** (1 John 3:22).
9. **We need to remain in Christ** (John 15:7).
10. **We should live in righteousness if we want God to grant our requests** (James 5:16; Psalm 34:15).

15 REASONS SUPPLICATIONS/PETITIONS ARE NOT GRANTED

1. **Unbelief** (James 1:6–8)
2. **Asking with wrong motivation/selfishness** (James 4:3)
3. **Harboring sinful attitudes/actions** (Psalm 66:18)
4. **Unconfessed sin** (Isaiah 59:1–2)
5. **Offering unworthy service to God** (Malachi 1:7–9)
6. **Wandering away from God** (Jeremiah 14:10)
7. **Ignoring the call of God** (Proverbs 1:24–25)
8. **Not hearing the law of God** (Proverbs 28:9)
9. **Ignoring the plight of the poor** (Proverbs 21:13)
10. **Idolatry in the heart** (Ezekiel 14:3; see also Jeremiah 11:11–14)

11. **Wavering in faith** (James 1:6–7)
12. **Hypocrisy** (Job 27:8–9)
13. **Pride** (Job 35:12–13)
14. **Self-righteousness** (Luke 18:11–12, 14)
15. **Lack of persistence** (1 Thessalonians 5:17)

BIBLICAL EXAMPLES OF GRANTED SUPPLICATIONS/PETITIONS

1. **Abraham** (Genesis 17:18, 20)
2. **Lot** (Genesis 19:18–21)
3. **Abraham's servant** (Genesis 24:15–27)
4. **Jacob** (Genesis 32:24–30)
5. **Israelites** (Exodus 2:23–24)
6. **Moses** (Exodus 17:4–6, 11–13)
7. **Samson** (Judges 15:16, 18–19)
8. **Hannah** (1 Samuel 1:22, 27)
9. **Samuel** (1 Samuel 7:9)
10. **Solomon** (1 Kings 3:6, 9–12)
11. **Man of God** (1 Kings 13:1, 6)
12. **Elijah** (1 Kings 18:36–38)
13. **Elisha** (2 Kings 4:32–35)
14. **Jehoahaz** (2 Kings 13:4)
15. **Hezekiah** (2 Kings 19:20)
16. **Jabez** (1 Chronicles 4:10)
17. **Asa** (2 Chronicles 14:11–12)
18. **Jehoshaphat** (2 Chronicles 20:5–17)
19. **Manasseh** (2 Chronicles 33:10–13, 19)
20. **Ezra** (Ezra 8:21–23)
21. **Nehemiah** (Nehemiah 4:9, 15)
22. **Job** (Job 42:10)
23. **David** (Psalm 18:6)
24. **Jeremiah** (Lamentations 3:55–56)
25. **Daniel** (Daniel 9:20–23)
26. **Jonah** (Jonah 2:2, 10)
27. **Zacharias** (Luke 1:13)
28. **Blind man** (Luke 18:35–43)
29. **Thief on the cross** (Luke 23:39–43)
30. **Apostles** (Acts 4:29–31)
31. **Cornelius** (Acts 10:1–4, 31)
32. **The early Christians** (Acts 12:5, 7)
33. **Paul and Silas** (Acts 16:25–26)

THANKSGIVING

God loves to answer His people's prayers, but He also loves to hear their words of appreciation for everything He has done for them. That includes the spiritual/heavenly blessings as well as the earthly/temporal ones.

10 BIBLICAL THINGS TO KNOW ABOUT THANKSGIVING

1. **The Bible commands it** (Psalm 50:14; Philippians 4:6).
2. **It should be offered regularly to God** (Psalm 50:14).
3. **It should be offered to Christ** (1 Timothy 1:12).
4. **It is to be offered through Christ** (Romans 1:8; Colossians 3:17; Hebrews 13:8, 15).
5. **It should be offered in private worship** (Daniel 6:10).
6. **It should be offered in public worship** (Psalm 35:18).
7. **It should be offered before meals** (John 6:11; Acts 27:35).
8. **It should be offered continuously** (Ephesians 1:16; 5:20; 1 Thessalonians 1:2).
9. **It should be offered for God's goodness and mercy** (Psalm 106:1; 107:1; 136:1–3).
10. **It should be part of prayer** (Philippians 4:6; Colossians 4:2).

11 THINGS TO BE THANKFUL FOR

1. **Christ's power** (Revelation 11:17)
2. **Freedom of sin through Christ** (Romans 7:23–25)
3. **The defeat of death** (1 Corinthians 15:55–57)
4. **The gift of wisdom** (Daniel 2:23)
5. **Converts** (Romans 6:17)
6. **The faith of others** (Romans 1:8; 2 Thessalonians 1:3)
7. **The love of others** (2 Thessalonians 1:3)
8. **God's grace on others** (1 Corinthians 1:4; Philippians 1:3–5; Colossians 1:3–7)
9. **God's nearness** (Psalm 75:1)
10. **God's provision for our needs** (Romans 14:6–7; 1 Timothy 4:3–4)
11. **Everything** (Ephesians 5:20)

BIBLICAL EXAMPLES OF THANKSGIVING

1. **David** (1 Chronicles 29:10, 13)
2. **Levites** (2 Chronicles 5:12–13)
3. **Daniel** (Daniel 2:20, 23)
4. **Jonah** (Jonah 2:1, 9)
5. **Simeon** (Luke 2:25–30)

6. **Anna** (Luke 2:36–38)
7. **Jesus** (Matthew 11:25; 26:26–27; John 6:11; 11:41)
8. **The apostle Paul** (Acts 28:15)

INTERCESSION

"Will you pray for me?" There may be no more honest, vulnerable question than this. When we show we are willing to pray for another, we draw closest to them—and to God—as we agree to petition Him to send that person His very best.

10 BIBLICAL THINGS TO KNOW ABOUT INTERCESSION

1. **It is commanded** (1 Timothy 2:1; James 5:14, 16).
2. **It is encouraged** (1 John 5:16).
3. **It is a sin to neglect it** (1 Samuel 12:23).
4. **It blesses the person praying** (Job 42:10).
5. **It is ineffective for the impenitent** (Jeremiah 7:13–16; 14:10–11).
6. **The Bible commands us to pray for all people** (1 Timothy 2:1).
7. **Jesus commanded His followers to pray for their enemies as well as for those who loved them** (Matthew 5:44).
8. **Jesus is our ultimate intercessor who still prays for us today** (Hebrews 7:22, 25).
9. **The word *intercession* literally means to "stand in the gap" for someone.**
10. **The apostle Paul encourages us to pray for all believers** (Ephesians 6:18).

PEOPLE/THINGS TO INTERCEDE FOR

1. **Those in authority** (1 Timothy 2:1–2)
2. **Ministers** (2 Corinthians 1:1, 11; Philippians 1:18–19)
3. **God's people/the Church** (Psalm 122:6; Isaiah 62:6–7; Ephesians 6:18)
4. **Children** (1 Samuel 1:27; Matthew 19:13)
5. **Friends** (Job 42:7–8)
6. **Fellow countrymen** (Romans 10:1)
7. **The sick** (James 5:14)
8. **Persecutors/enemies** (Matthew 5:44; Jeremiah 29:7)
9. **Those who forsake us** (2 Timothy 4:16)
10. **Those who complain against God** (Numbers 11:1; 14:19)
11. **By ministers for the people in their congregations** (Ephesians 1:16; 3:14–19; Philippians 1:4)

JESUS THE ULTIMATE INTERCESSOR

- **"But I have prayed for thee, that thy faith fail not:** and when thou art converted, strengthen thy brethren" (Luke 22:32).
- **"Then said Jesus, Father, forgive them; for they know not what they do.** And they parted his raiment, and cast lots" (Luke 23:34).
- **"I pray for them:** I pray not for the world, but for them which thou hast given me; for they are thine. And all mine are thine, and thine are mine; and I am glorified in them. And now I am no more in the world, but these are in the world, and I come to thee. Holy Father, keep through thine own name those whom thou hast given me, that they may be one, as we are. While I was with them in the world, I kept them in thy name: those that thou gavest me I have kept, and none of them is lost, but the son of perdition; that the scripture might be fulfilled. And now come I to thee; and these things I speak in the world, that they might have my joy fulfilled in themselves (John 17:9–13).
- **"Wherefore he is able also to save them to the uttermost that come unto God by him,** seeing he ever
liveth to make intercession for them (Hebrews 7:25).

18 BIBLICAL EXAMPLES OF INTERCESSION

1. **Abraham** (Genesis 18:23–32)
2. **Abraham's servant** (Genesis 24:12–14)
3. **Moses** (Exodus 8:12; 32:11–13)
4. **Samuel** (1 Samuel 7:5)
5. **King Solomon** (1 Kings 8:11, 30–36)
6. **Elisha** (2 Kings 4:32–33)
7. **King Hezekiah** (2 Chronicles 30:18)
8. **Isaiah** (2 Chronicles 32:20)
9. **Nehemiah** (Nehemiah 1:4–11)
10. **David** (Psalm 25:22)
11. **Ezekiel** (Ezekiel 9:8)
12. **Daniel** (Daniel 9:3–19)
13. **Stephen** (Acts 7:59–60)
14. **Peter and John** (Acts 8:14–15)
15. **Church of Jerusalem** (Acts 12:5)
16. **Paul** (Colossians 1:9–12; 2 Thessalonians 1:11)
17. **Epaphras** (Colossians 4:12)
18. **Philemon** (Philemon 1:1, 22)

3

From the Saints of Old
SOME BIBLICAL PRAYERS TO REMEMBER

ABRAHAM'S BARGAINING WITH GOD FOR SODOM

And the men turned their faces from thence, and went toward Sodom: but Abraham stood yet before the LORD. And Abraham drew near, and said, Wilt thou also destroy the righteous with the wicked? Peradventure there be fifty righteous within the city: wilt thou also destroy and not spare the place for the fifty righteous that are therein? That be far from thee to do after this manner, to slay the righteous with the wicked: and that the righteous should be as the wicked, that be far from thee: Shall not the Judge of all the earth do right? And the LORD said, If I find in Sodom fifty righteous within the city, then I will spare all the place for their sakes. And Abraham answered and said, Behold now, I have taken upon me to speak unto the LORD, which am but dust and ashes: Peradventure there shall lack five of the fifty righteous: wilt thou destroy all the city for lack of five? And he said, If I find there forty and five, I will not destroy it. And he spake unto him yet again, and said, Peradventure there shall be forty found there. And he said, I will not do it for forty's sake. And he said unto him, Oh let not the LORD be angry, and I will speak: Peradventure there shall thirty be found there. And he said, I will not do it, if I find thirty there. And he said, Behold now, I have taken upon me to speak unto the LORD: Peradventure there shall be twenty found there. And he said, I will not destroy it for twenty's sake. And he said, Oh let not the LORD be angry, and I will speak yet but this once: Peradventure ten shall be found there. And he said, I will not destroy it for ten's sake.

Genesis 18:22–32

JACOB PRAYS FOR MERCY FROM ESAU

And the messengers returned to Jacob, saying, We came to thy brother Esau, and also he cometh to meet thee, and four hundred men with him.

Then Jacob was greatly afraid and distressed: and he divided the people that was with him, and the flocks, and herds, and the camels, into two bands; and said, If Esau come to the one company, and smite it, then the other company which is left shall escape. And Jacob said, O God of my father Abraham, and God of my father Isaac, the LORD which saidst unto me, Return unto thy country, and to thy kindred, and I will deal well with thee: I am not worthy of the least of all the mercies, and of all the truth, which thou hast shewed unto thy servant; for with my staff I passed over this Jordan; and now I am become two bands.

Deliver me, I pray thee, from the hand of my brother, from the hand of Esau: for I fear him, lest he will come and smite me, and the mother with the children. And thou saidst, I will surely do thee good, and make thy seed as the sand of the sea, which cannot be numbered for multitude.

Genesis 32:6–12

JACOB PRAYS FOR A BLESSING AT PENIEL

And Jacob was left alone; and there wrestled a man with him until the breaking of the day. And when he saw that he prevailed not against him, he touched the hollow of his thigh; and the hollow of Jacob's thigh was out of joint, as he wrestled with him. and he said, Let me go, for the day breaketh. And he said, I will not let thee go, except thou bless me.

And he said unto him, What is thy name? And he said, Jacob. And he said, Thy name shall be called no more Jacob, but Israel: for as a prince hast thou power with God and with men, and hast prevailed.

And Jacob asked him, and said, Tell me, I pray thee, thy name. And he said, Wherefore is it that thou dost ask after my name? And he blessed him there. And Jacob called the name of the place Peniel: for I have seen God face to face, and my life is preserved.

Genesis 32:24–30

MOSES' PRAYER AT THE BURNING BUSH (ABRIDGED)

He said, I am the God of thy father, the God of Abraham, the God of Isaac, and the God of Jacob. And Moses hid his face; for he was afraid to look upon God. And the LORD said, I have surely seen the affliction of my people which are in Egypt, and have heard their cry by reason of their taskmasters; for I know their sorrows; and I am come down to deliver them out of the hand of the Egyptians, and to bring them up out of that land unto a good land and a large, unto a land flowing with milk and honey. . . . Come now therefore, and I will send thee unto Pharaoh, that thou mayest bring forth my people the children of Israel out of Egypt.

And Moses said unto God, Who am I, that I should go unto Pharaoh, and that I should bring forth the children of Israel out of Egypt? And he said, Certainly I will be with thee; and this shall be a token unto thee, that I have sent thee: When thou hast brought forth the people out of Egypt, ye shall serve God upon this mountain.

And Moses said unto God, Behold, when I come unto the children of Israel, and shall say unto them, The God of your fathers hath sent me unto you; and they shall say to me, What is his name? what shall I say unto them? And God said unto Moses, I AM THAT I AM: and he said, Thus shalt thou say unto the children of Israel, I AM hath sent me unto you. And God said moreover unto Moses, Thus shalt thou say unto the children of Israel, the LORD God of your fathers, the God of Abraham, the God of Isaac, and the God of Jacob, hath sent me unto you: this is my name for ever, and this is my memorial unto all generations.

Go, and gather the elders of Israel together, and say unto them, The LORD God of your fathers, the God of Abraham, of Isaac, and of Jacob, appeared unto me, saying, I have surely visited you, and seen that which is done to you in Egypt: And I have said, I will bring you up out of the affliction of Egypt. . .unto a land flowing with milk and honey. . . .

And I am sure that the king of Egypt will not let you go, no, not by a mighty hand. And I will stretch out my hand, and smite Egypt with all my wonders which I will do in the midst thereof: and after that he will let you go. And I will give this people favour in the sight of the Egyptians: and it shall come to pass, that, when ye go, ye shall not go empty.

But every woman shall borrow of her neighbour, and of her that sojourneth in her house, jewels of silver, and jewels of gold, and raiment: and ye shall put them upon your sons, and upon your daughters; and ye shall spoil the Egyptians.

And Moses answered and said, But, behold, they will not believe me, nor hearken unto my voice: for they will say, The LORD hath not appeared unto thee. And the LORD said unto him, What is that in thine hand? And he said, A rod. And he said, Cast it on the ground. And he cast it on the ground, and it became a serpent; and Moses fled from before it.

And the LORD said unto Moses, Put forth thine hand, and take it by the tail. And he put forth his hand, and caught it, and it became a rod in his hand: That they may believe that the LORD God of their fathers, the God of Abraham, the God of Isaac, and the God of Jacob, hath appeared unto thee.

And the LORD said furthermore unto him, Put now thine hand into thy bosom. And he put his hand into his bosom: and when he took it out, behold, his hand was leprous as snow. And he said, Put thine hand into thy bosom again. And he put his hand into his bosom again; and plucked it out of his bosom, and, behold, it was turned again as his other flesh.

And it shall come to pass, if they will not believe thee, neither hearken to the voice of the first sign, that they will believe the voice of the latter sign. And it shall come to pass, if they will not believe also these two signs, neither hearken unto thy voice, that thou shalt take of the water of the river, and pour it upon the dry land: and the water which thou takest out of the river shall become blood upon the dry land.

And Moses said unto the LORD, O my LORD, I am not eloquent, neither heretofore, nor since thou hast spoken unto thy servant: but I am slow of speech, and of a slow tongue.

And the LORD said unto him, Who hath made man's mouth? or who maketh the dumb, or deaf, or the seeing, or the blind? have not I the LORD? Now therefore go, and I will be with thy mouth, and teach thee what thou shalt say.

And he said, O my LORD, send, I pray thee, by the hand of him whom thou wilt send. And the anger of the LORD was kindled against Moses, and he said, Is not Aaron the Levite thy brother? I know that he can speak well. And also, behold, he cometh forth to meet thee: and when he seeth thee, he will be glad in his heart.

And thou shalt speak unto him, and put words in his mouth: and I will be with thy mouth, and with his mouth, and will teach you what ye shall do. And he shall be thy spokesman unto the people: and he shall be, even he shall be to thee instead of a mouth, and thou shalt be to him instead of God.

Complete prayer found in Exodus 3:1–4:18

MOSES' CONFESSION FOR ISRAEL IN THE WILDERNESS

And the LORD said unto Moses, I have seen this people, and, behold, it is a stiffnecked people: Now therefore let me alone, that my wrath may wax hot against them, and that I may consume them: and I will make of thee a great nation.

And Moses besought the LORD his God, and said, LORD, why doth thy wrath wax hot against thy people, which thou hast brought forth out of the land of Egypt with great power, and with a mighty hand? Wherefore should the Egyptians speak, and say, For mischief did he bring them out, to slay them in the mountains, and to consume them from the face of the earth? Turn from thy fierce wrath, and repent of this evil against thy people. Remember Abraham, Isaac, and Israel, thy servants, to whom thou swarest by thine own self, and saidst unto them, I will multiply your seed as the stars of heaven, and all this land that I have spoken of will I give unto your seed, and they shall inherit it for ever.

And the LORD repented of the evil which he thought to do unto his people.

Exodus 32:9–14

MOSES' PLEA FOR GOD'S PRESENCE

And Moses said unto the LORD, See, thou sayest unto me, Bring up this people: and thou hast not let me know whom thou wilt send with me. Yet thou hast said, I know thee by name, and thou hast also found grace in my sight.

Now therefore, I pray thee, if I have found grace in thy sight, shew me now thy way, that I may know thee, that I may find grace in thy sight: and consider that this nation is thy people.

And he said, My presence shall go with thee, and I will give thee rest.

And he said unto him, If thy presence go not with me, carry us not up hence. For wherein shall it be known here that I and thy people have found grace in thy sight? is it not in that thou goest with us? so shall we be separated, I and thy people, from all the people that are upon the face of the earth.

And the LORD said unto Moses, I will do this thing also that thou hast spoken: for thou hast found grace in my sight, and I know thee by name.

Exodus 33:12–17

JOSHUA'S PRAYER AFTER DEFEAT AT AI

And Joshua rent his clothes, and fell to the earth upon his face before the ark of the LORD until the eventide, he and the elders of Israel, and put dust upon their heads. And Joshua said, Alas, O LORD God, wherefore hast thou at all brought this people over Jordan, to deliver us into the hand of the Amorites, to destroy us? would to God we had been content, and dwelt on the other side Jordan! O LORD, what shall I say, when Israel turneth their backs before their enemies! For the Canaanites and all the inhabitants of the land shall hear of it, and shall environ us round, and cut off our name from the earth: and what wilt thou do unto thy great name?

And the LORD said unto Joshua, Get thee up; wherefore liest thou thus upon thy face? Israel hath sinned, and they have also transgressed my covenant which I commanded them: for they have even taken of the accursed thing, and have also stolen, and dissembled also, and they have put it even among their own stuff. Therefore the children of Israel could not stand before their enemies, but turned their backs before their enemies, because they were accursed: neither will I be with you any more, except ye destroy the accursed from among you.

Up, sanctify the people, and say, Sanctify yourselves against to morrow: for thus saith the LORD God of Israel, There is an accursed thing in the midst of thee, O Israel: thou canst not stand before thine enemies, until ye take away the accursed thing from among you. In the morning therefore ye shall be brought according to your tribes: and it shall be, that the tribe which the LORD taketh shall come according to the families thereof; and the family which the LORD shall take shall come by households; and the household which the LORD shall take shall come man by man.

And it shall be, that he that is taken with the accursed thing shall be burnt with fire, he and all that he hath: because he hath transgressed the covenant of the LORD, and because he hath wrought folly in Israel.

Joshua 7:6–15

HANNAH'S PRAYER FOR A CHILD

And she was in bitterness of soul, and prayed unto the LORD, and wept sore. And she vowed a vow, and said, O LORD of hosts, if thou wilt indeed look on the affliction of thine handmaid, and remember me, and not forget thine handmaid, but wilt give unto thine handmaid a man child, then I will give him unto the LORD all the days of his life, and there shall no razor come upon his head.

1 Samuel 1:10–11

SOLOMON'S REQUEST FOR WISDOM

And the king went to Gibeon to sacrifice there; for that was the great high place: a thousand burnt offerings did Solomon offer upon that altar. In Gibeon the LORD appeared to Solomon in a dream by night: and God said, Ask what I shall give thee.

And Solomon said, Thou hast shewed unto thy servant David my father great mercy, according as he walked before thee in truth, and in righteousness, and in uprightness of heart with thee; and thou hast kept for him this great kindness, that thou hast given him a son to sit on his throne, as it is this day. And now, O LORD my God, thou hast made thy servant king instead of David my father: and I am but a little child: I know not how to go out or come in. And thy servant is in the midst of thy people which thou hast chosen, a great people, that cannot be numbered nor counted for multitude.

Give therefore thy servant an understanding heart to judge thy people, that I may discern between good and bad: for who is able to judge this thy so great a people?

And the speech pleased the LORD, that Solomon had asked this thing.

And God said unto him, Because thou hast asked this thing, and hast not asked for thyself long life; neither hast asked riches for thyself, nor hast asked the life of thine enemies; but hast asked for thyself understanding to discern judgment; behold, I have done according to thy words: lo, I have given thee a wise and an understanding heart; so that there was none like thee before thee, neither after thee shall any arise like unto thee. And I have also given thee that which thou hast not asked, both riches, and honour: so that there shall not be any among the kings like unto thee all thy days.

And if thou wilt walk in my ways, to keep my statutes and my commandments, as thy father David did walk, then I will lengthen thy days.

1 Kings 3:4–14

HEZEKIAH'S PETITION FOR JUDAH'S DELIVERANCE

O LORD God of Israel, which dwellest between the cherubims, thou art the God, even thou alone, of all the kingdoms of the earth; thou hast made heaven and earth.

LORD, bow down thine ear, and hear: open, LORD, thine eyes, and see: and hear the words of Sennacherib, which hath sent him to reproach the living God.

Of a truth, LORD, the kings of Assyria have destroyed the nations and their lands, and have cast their gods into the fire: for they were no gods, but the work of men's hands, wood and stone: therefore they have destroyed them.

Now therefore, O LORD our God, I beseech thee, save thou us out of his hand, that all the kingdoms of the earth may know that thou art the LORD God, even thou only.

2 Kings 19:15–19

HEZEKIAH'S PLEA FOR HIS LIFE

Then he turned his face to the wall, and prayed unto the LORD, saying, I beseech thee, O LORD, remember now how I have walked before thee in truth and with a perfect heart, and have done that which is good in thy sight.

2 Kings 20:2–3

EZRA'S CONFESSION OF HIS PEOPLE'S SINS

O my God, I am ashamed and blush to lift up my face to thee, my God: for our iniquities are increased over our head, and our trespass is grown up unto the heavens.

Since the days of our fathers have we been in a great trespass unto this day; and for our iniquities have we, our kings, and our priests, been delivered into the hand of the kings of the lands, to the sword, to captivity, and to a spoil, and to confusion of face, as it is this day.

And now for a little space grace hath been shewed from the LORD our God, to leave us a remnant to escape, and to give us a nail in his holy place, that our God may lighten our eyes, and give us a little reviving in our bondage.

For we were bondmen; yet our God hath not forsaken us in our bondage, but hath extended mercy unto us in the sight of the kings of Persia, to give us a reviving, to set up the house of our God, and to repair the desolations thereof, and to give us a wall in Judah and in Jerusalem.

And now, O our God, what shall we say after this? for we have forsaken thy commandments, which thou hast commanded by thy servants the prophets, saying, The land, unto which ye go to possess it, is an unclean land with the filthiness of the people of the lands, with their abominations, which have filled it from one end to another with their uncleanness.

Now therefore give not your daughters unto their sons, neither take their daughters unto your sons, nor seek their peace or their wealth for ever: that ye may be strong, and eat the good of the land, and leave it for an inheritance to your children for ever.

And after all that is come upon us for our evil deeds, and for our great trespass, seeing that thou our God hast punished us less than our iniquities deserve, and hast given us such deliverance as this; should we again break thy commandments, and join in affinity with the people of these abominations? wouldest not thou be angry with us till thou hadst consumed us, so that there should be no remnant nor escaping?

O LORD God of Israel, thou art righteous: for we remain yet escaped, as it is this day: behold, we are before thee in our trespasses: for we cannot stand before thee because of this.

Ezra 9:6–15

Job's Prayer of Contrition

Then Job answered the LORD, and said, I know that thou canst do every thing, and that no thought can be withholden from thee. Who is he that hideth counsel without knowledge? therefore have I uttered that I understood not; things too wonderful for me, which I knew not.

Hear, I beseech thee, and I will speak: I will demand of thee, and declare thou unto me. I have heard of thee by the hearing of the ear: but now mine eye seeth thee. Wherefore I abhor myself, and repent in dust and ashes.

Job 42:1–6

David's Confession of Sin and Prayer for Pardon

Have mercy upon me, O God, according to thy lovingkindness: according unto the multitude of thy tender mercies blot out my transgressions. Wash me throughly from mine iniquity, and cleanse me from my sin. For I acknowledge my transgressions: and my sin is ever before me.

Against thee, thee only, have I sinned, and done this evil in thy sight: that thou mightest be justified when thou speakest, and be clear when thou judgest. Behold, I was shapen in iniquity; and in sin did my mother conceive me. Behold, thou desirest truth in the inward parts: and in the hidden part thou shalt make me to know wisdom.

Purge me with hyssop, and I shall be clean: wash me, and I shall be whiter than snow. Make me to hear joy and gladness; that the bones which thou hast broken may rejoice. Hide thy face from my sins, and blot out all mine iniquities.

Create in me a clean heart, O God; and renew a right spirit within me. Cast me not away from thy presence; and take not thy holy spirit from me. Restore unto me the joy of thy salvation; and uphold me with thy free spirit.

Psalm 51:1–12

David's Prayer for Deliverance

Deliver me, O LORD, from the evil man: preserve me from the violent man; which imagine mischiefs in their heart; continually are they gathered together for war. They have sharpened their tongues like a serpent; adders' poison is under their lips. Selah.

Keep me, O LORD, from the hands of the wicked; preserve me from the violent man; who have purposed to overthrow my goings. The proud have hid a snare for me, and cords; they have spread a net by the wayside; they have set gins for me. Selah.

I said unto the LORD, Thou art my God: hear the voice of my supplications, O LORD. O GOD the Lord, the strength of my salvation, thou hast covered my head in the day of battle. Grant not, O LORD, the desires of the wicked: further not his wicked device; lest they exalt themselves. Selah.

As for the head of those that compass me about, let the mischief of their own lips cover them. Let burning coals fall upon them: let them be cast into the fire; into deep pits, that they rise not up again. Let not an evil speaker be established in the earth: evil shall hunt the violent man to overthrow him.

I know that the LORD will maintain the cause of the afflicted, and the right of the poor. Surely the righteous shall give thanks unto thy name: the upright shall dwell in thy presence.

Psalm 140

ISAIAH'S PRAYER FOR MERCY

Oh that thou wouldest rend the heavens, that thou wouldest come down, that the mountains might flow down at thy presence, as when the melting fire burneth, the fire causeth the waters to boil, to make thy name known to thine adversaries, that the nations may tremble at thy presence!

When thou didst terrible things which we looked not for, thou camest down, the mountains flowed down at thy presence. For since the beginning of the world men have not heard, nor perceived by the ear, neither hath the eye seen, O God, beside thee, what he hath prepared for him that waiteth for him.

Thou meetest him that rejoiceth and worketh righteousness, those that remember thee in thy ways: behold, thou art wroth; for we have sinned: in those is continuance, and we shall be saved.

But we are all as an unclean thing, and all our righteousnesses are as filthy rags; and we all do fade as a leaf; and our iniquities, like the wind, have taken us away. And there is none that calleth upon thy name, that stirreth up himself to take hold of thee: for thou hast hid thy face from us, and hast consumed us, because of our iniquities.

But now, O LORD, thou art our father; we are the clay, and thou our potter; and we all are the work of thy hand. Be not wroth very sore, O LORD, neither remember iniquity for ever: behold, see, we beseech thee, we are all thy people.

Thy holy cities are a wilderness, Zion is a wilderness, Jerusalem a desolation. Our holy and our beautiful house, where our fathers praised thee, is burned up with fire: and all our pleasant things are laid waste.

Wilt thou refrain thyself for these things, O LORD? wilt thou hold thy peace, and afflict us very sore?

Isaiah 64

DANIEL'S CONFESSION ON BEHALF OF HIS PEOPLE

And I set my face unto the Lord God, to seek by prayer and supplications, with fasting, and sackcloth, and ashes: And I prayed unto the LORD my God, and made my confession, and said, O Lord, the great and dreadful God, keeping the covenant and mercy to them that love him, and to them that keep his commandments; we have sinned, and have committed iniquity, and have done wickedly, and have rebelled, even by departing from thy precepts and from thy judgments: neither have we hearkened unto thy servants the prophets, which spake in thy name to our kings, our princes, and our fathers, and to all the people of the land.

O LORD, righteousness belongeth unto thee, but unto us confusion of faces, as at this day; to the men of Judah, and to the inhabitants of Jerusalem, and unto all Israel, that are near, and that are far off, through all the countries whither thou hast driven them, because of their trespass that they have trespassed against thee. O Lord, to us belongeth confusion of face, to our kings, to our princes, and to our fathers, because we have sinned against thee.

To the Lord our God belong mercies and forgivenesses, though we have rebelled against him; neither have we obeyed the voice of the LORD our God, to walk in his laws, which he set before us by his servants the prophets.

Yea, all Israel have transgressed thy law, even by departing, that they might not obey thy voice; therefore the curse is poured upon us, and the oath that is written in the law of Moses the servant of God, because we have sinned against him.

And he hath confirmed his words, which he spake against us, and against our judges that judged us, by bringing upon us a great evil: for under the whole heaven hath not been done as hath been done upon Jerusalem. As it is written in the law of Moses, all this evil is come upon us: yet made we not our prayer before the LORD our God, that we might turn from our iniquities, and understand thy truth.

Therefore hath the LORD watched upon the evil, and brought it upon us: for the LORD our God is righteous in all his works which he doeth: for we obeyed not his voice. And now, O Lord our God, that hast brought thy people forth out of the land of Egypt with a mighty hand, and hast gotten thee renown, as at this day; we have sinned, we have done wickedly.

O LORD, according to all thy righteousness, I beseech thee, let thine anger and thy fury be turned away from thy city Jerusalem, thy holy mountain: because for our sins, and for the iniquities of our fathers, Jerusalem and thy people are become a reproach to all that are about us. Now therefore, O our God, hear the prayer of thy servant, and his supplications, and cause thy face to shine upon thy sanctuary that is desolate, for the Lord's sake.

O my God, incline thine ear, and hear; open thine eyes, and behold our desolations, and the city which is called by thy name: for we do not present our supplications before thee for our righteousnesses, but for thy great mercies.

O Lord, hear; O Lord, forgive; O Lord, hearken and do; defer not, for thine own sake, O my God: for thy city and thy people are called by thy name.

Daniel 9:3–19

JONAH'S CONTRITE PRAYER

I cried by reason of mine affliction unto the LORD, and he heard me; out of the belly of hell cried I, and thou heardest my voice. For thou hadst cast me into the deep, in the midst of the seas; and the floods compassed me about: all thy billows and thy waves passed over me.

Then I said, I am cast out of thy sight; yet I will look again toward thy holy temple. The waters compassed me about, even to the soul: the depth closed me round about, the weeds were wrapped about my head.

I went down to the bottoms of the mountains; the earth with her bars was about me for ever: yet hast thou brought up my life from corruption, O LORD my God. When my soul fainted within me I remembered the LORD: and my prayer came in unto thee, into thine holy temple.

They that observe lying vanities forsake their own mercy. But I will sacrifice unto thee with the voice of thanksgiving; I will pay that that I have vowed. Salvation is of the LORD.

Jonah 2:2–9

HABAKKUK'S PRAYER QUESTIONING GOD

O LORD, how long shall I cry, and thou wilt not hear! even cry out unto thee of violence, and thou wilt not save! Why dost thou shew me iniquity, and cause me to behold grievance? for spoiling and violence are before me: and there are that raise up strife and contention.

Therefore the law is slacked, and judgment doth never go forth: for the wicked doth compass about the righteous; therefore wrong judgment proceedeth. Behold ye among the heathen, and regard, and wonder marvelously: for I will work a work in your days which ye will not believe, though it be told you.

For, lo, I raise up the Chaldeans, that bitter and hasty nation, which shall march through the breadth of the land, to possess the dwellingplaces that are not theirs. They are terrible and dreadful: their judgment and their dignity shall proceed of themselves. Their horses also are swifter than the leopards, and are more fierce than the evening wolves: and their horsemen shall spread themselves, and their horsemen shall come from far; they shall fly as the eagle that hasteth to eat. They shall come all for violence: their faces shall sup up as the east wind, and they shall gather the captivity as the sand. And they shall scoff at the kings, and the princes shall be a scorn unto them: they shall deride every strong hold; for they shall heap dust, and take it.

Then shall his mind change, and he shall pass over, and offend, imputing this his power unto his god. Art thou not from everlasting, O LORD my God, mine Holy One? we shall not die. O LORD, thou hast ordained them for judgment; and, O mighty God, thou hast established them for correction.

Thou art of purer eyes than to behold evil, and canst not look on iniquity: wherefore lookest thou upon them that deal treacherously, and holdest thy tongue when the wicked devoureth the man that is more righteous than he? And makest men as the fishes of the sea, as the creeping things, that have no ruler over them?

They take up all of them with the angle, they catch them in their net, and gather them in their drag: therefore they rejoice and are glad. Therefore they sacrifice unto their net, and burn incense unto their drag; because by them their portion is fat, and their meat plenteous. Shall they therefore empty their net, and not spare continually to slay the nations?

I will stand upon my watch, and set me upon the tower, and will watch to see what he will say unto me, and what I shall answer when I am reproved.

Habakkuk 1:2–2:1

HABAKKUK'S PRAYER OF PRAISE

O LORD, I have heard thy speech, and was afraid: O LORD, revive thy work in the midst of the years, in the midst of the years make known; in wrath remember mercy. God came from Teman, and the Holy One from mount Paran. Selah. His glory covered the heavens, and the earth was full of his praise. And his brightness was as the light; he had horns coming out of his hand: and there was the hiding of his power. Before him went the pestilence, and burning coals went forth at his feet.

He stood, and measured the earth: he beheld, and drove asunder the nations; and the everlasting mountains were scattered, the perpetual hills did bow: his ways are everlasting. I saw the tents of Cushan in affliction: and the curtains of the land of Midian did tremble.

Was the LORD displeased against the rivers? was thine anger against the rivers? was thy wrath against the sea, that thou didst ride upon thine horses and thy chariots of salvation? Thy bow was made quite naked, according to the oaths of the tribes, even thy word. Selah. Thou didst cleave the earth with rivers.

The mountains saw thee, and they trembled: the overflowing of the water passed by: the deep uttered his voice, and lifted up his hands on high.

The sun and moon stood still in their habitation: at the light of thine arrows they went, and at the shining of thy glittering spear. Thou didst march through the land in indignation, thou didst thresh the heathen in anger. Thou wentest forth for the salvation of thy people, even for salvation with thine anointed; thou woundedst the head out of the house of the wicked, by discovering the foundation unto the neck. Selah.

Thou didst strike through with his staves the head of his villages: they came out as a whirlwind to scatter me: their rejoicing was as to devour the poor secretly. Thou didst walk through the sea with thine horses, through the heap of great waters.

When I heard, my belly trembled; my lips quivered at the voice: rottenness entered into my bones, and I trembled in myself, that I might rest in the day of trouble: when he cometh up unto the people, he will invade them with his troops.

Although the fig tree shall not blossom, neither shall fruit be in the vines; the labour of the olive shall fail, and the fields shall yield no meat; the flock shall be cut off from the fold, and there shall be no herd in the stalls: Yet I will rejoice in the LORD, I will joy in the God of my salvation.

The LORD God is my strength, and he will make my feet like hinds' feet, and he will make me to walk upon mine high places.

Habakkuk 3:2–19

JESUS' "HIGH PRIESTLY" PRAYER
See chapter 1, page 27

JESUS' PRAYER AT GETHSEMANE
See chapter 1, page 27
(Matthew 26:36–42)

THE CHURCH'S PRAYER FOR BOLDNESS
And when they heard that, they lifted up their voice to God with one accord, and said, Lord, thou art God, which hast made heaven, and earth, and the sea, and all that in them is: Who by the mouth of thy servant David hast said, Why did the heathen rage, and the people imagine vain things?

The kings of the earth stood up, and the rulers were gathered together against the Lord, and against his Christ. For of a truth against thy holy child Jesus, whom thou hast anointed, both Herod, and Pontius Pilate, with the Gentiles, and the people of Israel, were gathered together, for to do whatsoever thy hand and thy counsel determined before to be done.

And now, Lord, behold their threatenings: and grant unto thy servants, that with all boldness they may speak thy word, by stretching forth thine hand to heal; and that signs and wonders may be done by the name of thy holy child Jesus.

And when they had prayed, the place was shaken where they were assembled together; and they were all filled with the Holy Ghost, and they spake the word of God with boldness.

Acts 4:24–31

STEPHEN, AS HE WAS MARTYRED
And he kneeled down, and cried with a loud voice, Lord, lay not this sin to their charge. And when he had said this, he fell asleep.

Acts 7:60

THE APOSTLE PAUL, FOR THE EPHESIANS

Wherefore I also, after I heard of your faith in the Lord Jesus, and love unto all the saints, cease not to give thanks for you, making mention of you in my prayers; that the God of our Lord Jesus Christ, the Father of glory, may give unto you the spirit of wisdom and revelation in the knowledge of him: the eyes of your understanding being enlightened; that ye may know what is the hope of his calling, and what the riches of the glory of his inheritance in the saints, and what is the exceeding greatness of his power to us-ward who believe, according to the working of his mighty power, which he wrought in Christ, when he raised him from the dead, and set him at his own right hand in the heavenly places, far above all principality, and power, and might, and dominion, and every name that is named, not only in this world, but also in that which is to come: and hath put all things under his feet, and gave him to be the head over all things to the church, which is his body, the fulness of him that filleth all in all. . . .

For this cause I bow my knees unto the Father of our Lord Jesus Christ, of whom the whole family in heaven and earth is named, That he would grant you, according to the riches of his glory, to be strengthened with might by his Spirit in the inner man; that Christ may dwell in your hearts by faith; that ye, being rooted and grounded in love, may be able to comprehend with all saints what is the breadth, and length, and depth, and height; and to know the love of Christ, which passeth knowledge, that ye might be filled with all the fulness of God.

Now unto him that is able to do exceeding abundantly above all that we ask or think, according to the power that worketh in us, unto him be glory in the church by Christ Jesus throughout all ages, world without end. Amen.

Ephesians 1:15–23; 3:14–21

4

Jesus: The Ultimate Man of Prayer
CHRIST'S TEACHING AND EXAMPLE IN PRAYER

As the Son of God—God in "the flesh," as the Bible puts it—no one has ever had a better understanding of what prayer is, what it's for, and what it does than the Lord Jesus Christ. Jesus was completely and perfectly "in tune" with His heavenly Father, and He stayed that way through a life of perfect prayer.

Jesus prayed perfectly, and He also gave His followers the best teaching on prayer anyone has ever heard.

JESUS' TEACHINGS ON PRAYER

- **Pray for those who mistreat you:** "I say unto you, Love your enemies, bless them that curse you, do good to them that hate you, and pray for them which despitefully use you, and persecute you" (Matthew 5:44).
- **Don't pray in public so others will see you:** "And when thou prayest, thou shalt not be as the hypocrites are: for they love to pray standing in the synagogues and in the corners of the streets, that they may be seen of men. Verily I say unto you, They have their reward" (Matthew 6:5).
- **Pray in private, knowing that God will reward you:** "But thou, when thou prayest, enter into thy closet, and when thou hast shut thy door, pray to thy Father which is in secret; and thy Father which seeth in secret shall reward thee openly" (Matthew 6:6).
- **Don't pray using repetition:** "But when ye pray, use not vain repetitions, as the heathen do: for they think that they shall be heard for their much speaking" (Matthew 6:7).
- **Pray knowing that God hears and knows what you need:** "Your Father knoweth what things ye have need of, before ye ask him" (Matthew 6:8).
- **The Model Prayer:** "After this manner therefore pray ye: Our Father which art in heaven, Hallowed be thy name. Thy kingdom come, Thy will be done in earth, as it is in heaven. Give us this day our daily bread. And forgive us our debts, as we forgive our debtors. And lead us not into temptation, but deliver us from evil: For thine is the kingdom, and the power, and the glory, for ever. Amen" (Matthew 6:9–13).
- **Pray that God will send workers out to win souls:** "Pray ye therefore the Lord of the harvest, that he will send forth labourers into his harvest" (Matthew 9:38).
- **Prayer and fasting are sometimes necessary in spiritual battle:**

"Howbeit this kind goeth not out but by prayer and fasting" (Matthew 17:21, see also Mark 9:29).

- **Believing God is necessary for receiving from God:** "And all things, whatsoever ye shall ask in prayer, believing, ye shall receive" (Matthew 21:22).
- **Pray to fight temptation:** "Watch and pray, that ye enter not into temptation: the spirit indeed is willing, but the flesh is weak" (Matthew 26:41).
- **When you pray, forgive others:** "And when ye stand praying, forgive, if ye have ought against any: that your Father also which is in heaven may forgive you your trespasses" (Mark 11:25).
- **Jesus' own authority in prayer:** "Thinkest thou that I cannot now pray to my Father, and he shall presently give me more than twelve legions of angels?" (Matthew 26:53).

JESUS' PARABLES ON PRAYER

During His earthly ministry, Jesus often taught using parables—stories that made a point about the kingdom of God. Two of those parables dealt extensively with prayer and the part it would play in the disciples' lives—and in the lives of believers who followed them. The first, which is listed in Luke 18:1–8, deals with persistence in prayer, while the second, found in Luke 18:9–14, deals with the proper attitude of humility during prayer.

PARABLE OF THE PERSISTENT WIDOW (LUKE 18:1–8)

And he spake a parable unto them to this end, that men ought always to pray, and not to faint; saying, There was in a city a judge, which feared not God, neither regarded man: And there was a widow in that city; and she came unto him, saying, Avenge me of mine adversary.

And he would not for a while: but afterward he said within himself, Though I fear not God, nor regard man; yet because this widow troubleth me, I will avenge her, lest by her continual coming she weary me.

And the Lord said, Hear what the unjust judge saith. And shall not God avenge his own elect, which cry day and night unto him, though he bear long with them? I tell you that he will avenge them speedily. Nevertheless when the Son of man cometh, shall he find faith on the earth?

PARABLE OF THE PHARISEE AND THE TAX COLLECTOR (LUKE 18:9–14)

And he spake this parable unto certain which trusted in themselves that they were righteous, and despised others: Two men went up into the temple to pray; the one a Pharisee, and the other a publican. The Pharisee stood and prayed thus with himself, God, I thank thee, that I am not as other men are, extortioners, unjust, adulterers, or even as this publican. I fast twice in the week, I give tithes of all that I possess.

And the publican, standing afar off, would not lift up so much as his eyes unto heaven, but smote upon his breast, saying, God be merciful to me a sinner.

I tell you, this man went down to his house justified rather than the other; for every one that exalteth himself shall be abased; and he that humbleth himself shall be exalted.

MORE ON THE "MODEL PRAYER," ALSO KNOWN AS "THE LORD'S PRAYER"

Jesus didn't intend for His followers to simply recite what has come to be known as the "Lord's verbatim"; instead, He simply wanted them to remember this prayer so they could use it as a model for effective, life-changing interaction with God.

Here is the significance of the Lord's Prayer, line by line:

- **"Our Father which art in heaven":** This acknowledges God's true place while at the same time addressing Him as a personal heavenly Father.
- **"Hallowed be thy name":** This refers to the praise and worship that is due Him.
- **"Thy kingdom come, Thy will be done in earth, as it is in heaven":** This is a prayer of dependency and of submission to the will of God.
- **"Give us this day our daily bread":** We are to make our requests known to God and ask for daily provision.
- **"And forgive us our debts":** Confession of sin should be a part of any effective prayer to God.
- **"As we forgive our debtors":** It is important to God that His people forgive one another for any wrongs done.
- **"And lead us not into temptation, but deliver us from evil":** We are to pray for help in facing up to the trials and temptations that the devil and the world bring our way.

JESUS ALSO PRAYED FOR:

- **Children** (Matthew 19:13–14)
- **Himself and His mission on earth** (Matthew 26:36–44)
- **The apostle Peter** (Luke 22:31–32)
- **His disciples** (John 17:9–15)
- **Future believers** (John 17:20)
- **The coming of the Holy Spirit** (John 16:25–27)

PLACES JESUS PRAYED

- **A mountain** (Matthew 14:23; Mark 6:46; Luke 6:12)

- **The Mount of Transfiguration** (Luke 9:28–36)
- **A "solitary place"** (Mark 1:35)
- **The Garden of Gethsemane** (Matthew 26:36–45; Luke 22:41)
- **The wilderness** (Luke 5:16)

JESUS' RECORDED PRAYERS

- **His prayer at Lazarus's tomb:** "Father, I thank thee that thou hast heard me. And I knew that thou hearest me always: but because of the people which stand by I said it, that they may believe that thou hast sent me" (John 11:41–42).
- "I thank thee, O Father, Lord of heaven and earth, because thou hast hid these things from the wise and prudent, and hast revealed them unto babes. Even so, Father: for so it seemed good in thy sight" (Matthew 11:25–26; see also Luke 10:21).
- **His prayer as his death approached:** "Now is my soul troubled; and what shall I say? Father, save me from this hour: but for this cause came I unto this hour. Father, glorify thy name" (John 12:27–28).

JESUS' HIGH PRIESTLY PRAYER (JOHN 17:1–26)

Jesus Prays for Himself

Father, the hour is come; glorify thy Son, that thy Son also may glorify thee: As thou hast given him power over all flesh, that he should give eternal life to as many as thou hast given him. And this is life eternal, that they might know thee the only true God, and Jesus Christ, whom thou hast sent.

I have glorified thee on the earth: I have finished the work which thou gavest me to do. And now, O Father, glorify thou me with thine own self with the glory which I had with thee before the world was.

Jesus Prays for His Disciples

I have manifested thy name unto the men which thou gavest me out of the world: thine they were, and thou gavest them me; and they have kept thy word. Now they have known that all things whatsoever thou hast given me are of thee.

For I have given unto them the words which thou gavest me; and they have received them, and have known surely that I came out from thee, and they have believed that thou didst send me. I pray for them: I pray not for the world, but for them which thou hast given me; for they are thine. And all mine are thine, and thine are mine; and I am glorified in them.

And now I am no more in the world, but these are in the world, and I come to thee. Holy Father, keep through thine own name those whom thou hast given me, that they may be one, as we are. While I was with them in the world, I kept them in thy name: those that thou gavest me I have kept, and none of them is lost, but the son of perdition; that the scripture might be fulfilled.

And now come I to thee; and these things I speak in the world, that they might have my joy fulfilled in themselves. I have given them thy word; and the world hath hated them, because they are not of the world, even as I am not of the world.

I pray not that thou shouldest take them out of the world, but that thou shouldest keep them from the evil. They are not of the world, even as I am not of the world. Sanctify them through thy truth: thy word is truth. As thou hast sent me into the world, even so have I also sent them into the world. And for their sakes I sanctify myself, that they also might be sanctified through the truth.

Jesus Prays for All Believers

Neither pray I for these alone, but for them also which shall believe on me through their word; that they all may be one; as thou, Father, art in me, and I in thee, that they also may be one in us: that the world may believe that thou hast sent me.

And the glory which thou gavest me I have given them; that they may be one, even as we are one: I in them, and thou in me, that they may be made perfect in one; and that the world may know that thou hast sent me, and hast loved them, as thou hast loved me.

Father, I will that they also, whom thou hast given me, be with me where I am; that they may behold my glory, which thou hast given me: for thou lovedst me before the foundation of the world.

O righteous Father, the world hath not known thee: but I have known thee, and these have known that thou hast sent me. And I have declared unto them thy name, and will declare it: that the love wherewith thou hast loved me may be in them, and I in them.

JESUS' PRAYERS AT GETHSEMANE

- "O my Father, if it be possible, let this cup pass from me: nevertheless not as I will, but as thou wilt" (Matthew 26:39).
- "O my Father, if this cup may not pass away from me, except I drink it, thy will be done" (Matthew 26:42).
- "Abba, Father, all things are possible unto thee; take away this cup from me: nevertheless not what I will, but what thou wilt" (Mark 14:36).
- "Father, if thou be willing, remove this cup from me: nevertheless not my will, but thine, be done" (Luke 22:42).

Jesus' Prayers from the Cross

- "Father, forgive them; for they know not what they do" (Luke 23:34).
- "My God, my God, why hast thou forsaken me?" (Matthew 27:46; Mark 15:34).
- "It is finished" (John 19:30).
- "Father, into thy hands I commend my spirit" (Luke 23:46).

5

Some Great Sayings about Prayer
QUOTATIONS FROM PRAYING
MEN AND WOMEN

GENERAL QUOTATIONS

The purpose of prayer is to get God's will done.

Samuel Gordon
Quiet Talks on Prayer (1904)

I must pour out my heart in the language which His Spirit gives me; and more than that, I must trust in the Spirit to speak the unutterable groanings of my spirit, when my lips cannot actually express all the emotions of my heart.

Charles Spurgeon
"The Fatherhood of God" sermon (1858)

Every day you have another opportunity to affect your future with the words you speak to God.

Stormie Omartian
Just Enough Light for the Step I'm On (1999)

Sometimes a person prays with his tears, even when words are missing.

Bill Gothard
The Power of Crying Out (2002)

Daily prayer for daily needs.

E. M. Bounds
The Necessity of Prayer (19th century)

Faith thrives in an atmosphere of prayer.

E. M. Bounds
The Necessity of Prayer (19th century)

He prays not at all, who does not press his plea.

E. M. Bounds
The Necessity of Prayer (19th century)

Humility is an indispensable requisite of true prayer.

E. M. Bounds
The Essentials of Prayer (19th century)

Humility must be in the praying character as light is in the sun.

E. M. Bounds
The Essentials of Prayer (19th century)

Kneeling well becomes us as the attitude of prayer, because it betokens humility.

E. M. Bounds
The Essentials of Prayer (19th century)

What a nobility would come into life if secret prayer were not only an asking for some new sense of comfort, or light, or strength, but the giving a way of life just for one day into the sure and safe keeping of a mighty and faithful God.

Andrew Murray
The Prayer Life (1912)

Every day is a good day if you pray.

Norman Vincent Peale
The Power of Positive Thinking (1952)

When we feel least like praying is the time when we most need to pray.

R. A. Torrey
How to Pray (1900)

The prayer that is born of meditation upon the Word of God is the prayer that soars upward most easily to God's listening ear.

R. A. Torrey
How to Pray (1900)

There is no question God will duck, no battle He can't win, no topic He doesn't know. You can't make Him uncomfortable. You can't push Him too hard. So go ahead, hit Him with your best shot.

Karon Phillips Goodman
You're Late Again, Lord! (2002)

Unless the common course of our lives be according to the common spirit of our prayers, our prayers are so far from being real or sufficient degree of devotion that they become an empty lip-labor, or, what is worse, a notorious hypocrisy.

William Law
A Serious Call to a Devout and Holy Life (1729)

Let not the understanding, but the whole heart set upon the living God as the teacher, be the chief thing, when thou enterest thy closet. Then shalt thou find good understanding. God will give thee an understanding heart, a spiritual understanding.

Andrew Murray
Prayer's Inner Chamber (1912)

My prayers, my God, flow from what I am not; I think Thy answers make me what I am.

George MacDonald
Diary of an Old Soul (1880)

Look deep, yet deeper, in my heart, and there, beyond where I can feel, read thou the prayer.

George MacDonald
Diary of an Old Soul (1880)

Where I am most perplexed, it may be there Thou mak'st a secret chamber, holy-dim, where Thou wilt come to help my deepest prayer.

George MacDonald
Diary of an Old Soul (1880)

Remember, the shortest distance between a problem and the solution is the distance between our knees and the floor.

Charles Stanley
Handle with Prayer (1987)

Prayer allows a place for me to bring my doubts and complaints and subject them to the blinding light of reality I cannot comprehend but can haltingly learn to trust.

Philip Yancey
Prayer: Does It Make Any Difference? (2006)

Most of us talk too much when we pray, which is really kind of silly when you think about it. If prayer is a conversation with God, how can we hear what He has to say if we're talking all the time?

Bob Buford
Game Plan (1997)

The benefits of prayer come not from praying but from living what we discover in prayer.

Matthew Kelly
A Call to Joy (1997)

When we can't pray, when the words won't come, when we don't know what to pray for, we have the Spirit within us, who prays for us. What an honor, what a privilege, what a gift. And what a God, who would make such provision for us!

Ray Pritchard
The God You Can Trust (2003)

Prayer is so universal and so natural that its place in our lives needs no defense. We all pray, and we pray because it is a part of our nature.

Robert and Debra Bruce
Reclaiming Intimacy (1996)

When people love one another, they pray for one another, and when they pray for one another, they learn to love one another more deeply.

Glenn Daman
Shepherding the Small Church (2002)

What we want is to press our case right up to the throne of God.

D. L. Moody
Prevailing Prayer: What Hinders It? (1884)

All true prayer must be offered in full submission to God.

D. L. Moody
Prevailing Prayer: What Hinders It? (1884)

To pray and not act is not only deception but also plain laziness.

Scott Hinkle
Recapturing the Primary Purpose (2005)

When we practice a rule of prayer, prayer gradually becomes a holy habit, something we do that is not dependent on feelings or moods or our ability to articulate well. It becomes central to our lives and strengthens our connections to God.

Valerie Hess and Marti Watson Garlett
Habits of a Child's Heart (2004)

If we are unwilling to change, we will abandon prayer as a noticeable characteristic of our lives.

Richard Foster
Celebration of Discipline (1978)

Fretting magnifies the *problem*, but prayer magnifies *God*.

Joanna Weaver
Having a Mary Heart in a Martha World (2000)

Prayer never evaporates.

Elisabeth Elliot
The Music of His Promises (2000)

Sometimes we need to pray about what to pray about.

Virginia Ann Froehle
Loving Yourself More (1993)

Prayer is not trying to manipulate God into doing our will.

Steve Campbell
"Foundations for Answered Prayer" sermon (2009)

Not that you should imagine that the purpose of your prayer is to tell the Lord what you want; for He knows well enough what you need. Rather, the purpose of prayer is to make you ready and able to receive as a clean vessel the grace that our Lord would freely give to you.

Walter Hilton
Toward a Perfect Love (1985)

Every day as we have prayed, "Thy kingdom come," has our Christian consciousness taken in the tremendous sweep of that prayer and seen how it covers the length and breadth of this great world and every interest of human life?

Henry Drummond
A Life for a Life and Other Addresses
(1893)

When we pray more we can talk less.

A. W. Tozer "In Everything by Prayer" sermon (20th century)

Ask God to open your heart and kindle in it a spark of His love, and then you will begin to understand what praying means.

Jean-Nicholas Grou
How to Pray (18th century)

Why do we pray so much with our lips and so little with our heart?

Jean-Nicholas Grou
How to Pray (18th century)

PRAYER AS DEPENDENCE UPON GOD

True prayer is a spontaneous outpouring of honesty and need from the soul's foundation. In calm times, we say a prayer. In desperate times, we truly *pray*.

David Jeremiah
A Bend in the Road (2000)

True prayers are born of present trials and present needs.

E. M. Bounds
The Necessity of Prayer (19th century)

Prayer shows our dependence on God. It honors Him as the source of all blessing, and it reminds us that converting individuals and growing churches are His works, not ours.

Mark Dever and Paul Alexander
The Deliberate Church (2005)

Prayer is a declaration of our dependence on God. It isn't something mechanical you do; it is somewhere you go to meet Someone you know.

Jill Briscoe
The New Normal (2005)

The very thing that most qualifies us to pray is our helplessness.

David Jeremiah
The Prayer Matrix (2004)

Make no decision without prayer.

Elizabeth George
A Woman after God's Own Heart (1997)

Helplessness united with faith produces prayer.

O. Hallesby
Prayer (1931)

When all other courses of action have been eliminated, when we stand on the edge of the abyss, when we approach God with empty hands and an aching heart, then we draw close to the true heart of prayer.

Jerry Sittser
When God Doesn't Answer Your Prayer (2003)

The prayer of a Christian is not an attempt to force God's hand, but a humble acknowledgment of helplessness and dependence.

J. I. Packer
Evangelism and the Sovereignty of God (2008)

Prayers are needed. They are the winged messengers to carry the need to God.

John Wright Follette
Broken Bread (1957)

PRAYER AS COMMUNION WITH GOD

God knows what's in our hearts. We might as well get right to the point.

Bruce Bickel and Stan Jantz
God Is in the Small Stuff (1998)

In prayer man rises to heaven to dwell with God: in the Word God comes to dwell with man. In prayer man gives himself to God: in the Word God gives Himself to man.

Andrew Murray
The Prayer Life (1912)

The least little remembrance will always be acceptable to Him. You need not cry very loud.

Brother Lawrence
The Practice of the Presence of God (17th century)

Prayer provides nourishment for your soul, satiates that "inner" spiritual hunger, and helps you develop your relationship with a loving Father who can heal distraught relationships.

Robert and Debra Bruce
Reclaiming Intimacy (1996)

Most of us don't pray on a regular basis because we're aware it will cost us something. . .honesty.

Jack Hayford
Prayer Is Invading the Impossible (2002)

Prayer is not to get the goods. It is to enjoy the One who is good.

Jon Courson
Application Commentary (2003)

The great gift of God in prayer is Himself.

Maxie Dunnam
The Workbook of Intercessory Prayer (1979)

His prayer was nothing else but a sense of the presence of God.

Brother Lawrence
The Practice of the Presence of God (17th century)

To pray is to let Jesus into our lives.

O. Hallesby
Prayer (1931)

It is through prayer that we become friends with Christ.

Matthew Kelly
A Call to Joy (1997)

Thy praying voice is music in God's ears.

Matthew Henry
Commentary on the Whole Bible (1706)

I challenge you to shift the focus of your prayer. Don't spend a lot of time describing your mountain to the Lord. He knows what it is. Instead, focus your attention on the mountain mover—His glory, power, and faithfulness.

Bill Hybels
Too Busy Not to Pray (1988)

Prayer is our being in a constant state of understanding that we are in His presence, talking with Him as we would a friend—a father—and being ever intent on hearing His voice as He speaks to us.

Eva Marie Everson
Oasis (2007)

The call to unceasing prayer is not an invitation to divided consciousness; it does not imply that we pay any less attention to daily realities or retreat from life's responsibilities. . .[It] means being consciously constantly conscious of the presence of God amidst the changing complexion of everyday life.

Debra Farrington
Unceasing Prayer: A Beginner's Guide
(2002)

The purpose of prayer is not primarily to move the hand of God but rather to hold the hand of God.

Jon Courson
Application Commentary (2006)

So many times we try to please God by the length of time we pray. Legislating prayer time becomes as unnatural as legislating conversations or hugs or kisses.

Steve Sampson
You Can Hear the Voice of God (1993)

Some people think God does not like to be troubled with our constant coming and asking. The only way to trouble God is not to come at all.

D. L. Moody
Prevailing Prayer: What Hinders It? (1884)

When we pray it is far more important to pray with a sense of the greatness of God than with a sense of the greatness of the problem.

Gordon Jackson
Destination Unknown (2004)

When the appointed times of prayer were past, he found no difference, because he still continued with God, praising and blessing Him with all his might, so that he passed his life in continual joy.

Brother Lawrence
The Practice of the Presence of God (17th century)

A little lifting up the heart suffices; a little remembrance of God, one act of inward worship, though upon a march, and sword in hand, are prayers which however short, are nevertheless very acceptable to God.

Brother Lawrence
The Practice of the Presence of God (17th century)

Prayer is related to our inborn hunger for God. And prayer is not for God's benefit, but for ours.

Robert and Debra Bruce
Reclaiming Intimacy (1996)

The heart has been poured out, and now lifted upon the wings of prayer the message is wafted up and away through the silent reaches of space to the Father's throne.

John Wright Follette
Broken Bread (1957)

Why do we not lay open our heart to God and beg Him to put into it whatever is most pleasing to Him?

Jean-Nicholas Grou
How to Pray (18 th century)

The determined fixing of our will upon God, and pressing toward Him steadily and without deflection; this is the very center and the art of prayer.

Evelyn Underhill
The Essentials of Mysticism (1960)

Prayer, then, begins by an intellectual adjustment. By thinking of God earnestly and humbly to the exclusion of other objects of thought, by deliberately surrendering the mind to spiritual things, by preparing the consciousness for the inflow of new life.

Evelyn Underhill
The Essentials of Mysticism (1960)

An open life, an open hand, open upward, is the pipeline of communication between the heart of God and this poor befooled old world.

Samuel Gordon
Quiet Talks on Prayer (1904)

The essence of prayer is simply talking to God as you would to a beloved friend—without pretense or flippancy.

John MacArthur
Alone with God (1995)

I think of praying at all times as living in continual God-consciousness, where everything we see and experience becomes a kind of prayer, lived in deep awareness of and surrender to our heavenly Father.

John MacArthur
Alone with God (1995)

THE POWER OF PRAYER

Prayer and faith are sacred picklocks that can open secrets and obtain great treasures.

Charles Spurgeon
"The Holy Ghost—The Great Teacher" sermon (1855)

Prayer is the never-failing resort of the Christian in any case and in every plight.

Charles Spurgeon
"The Believer Sinking in the Mire" sermon (1865)

Prayer isn't getting your way in heaven; it's getting God's way on earth.

Greg Laurie
Wrestling with God (2003)

More can be accomplished in prayer in the first hours of the day than at any other time during the day.

R. A. Torrey
How to Pray (1900)

If we are to pray with power we must pray *with faith*.

R. A. Torrey
How to Pray (1900)

Nights of prayer to God are followed by days of power with men.

R. A. Torrey
How to Pray (1900)

God will use our simple prayers because of the authority behind them.

Rich Mendola
"The Acts of the Holy Spirit: Wonders and Good News" sermon (2009)

Prayer should be the means by which I, at all times, receive all that I need, and, for this reason, be my daily refuge, my daily consolation, my daily joy, my source of rich and inexhaustible joy in life.

O. Hallesby
Prayer (1931)

Someone has said that when we work, *we* work; but when we pray, *God* works. His supernatural strength is available to praying people who are convinced to the core of their beings that He can make a difference.

Bill Hybels
Too Busy Not to Pray (1988)

Scripture insists that God has hardwired the universe in such a way that He works primarily through prayer.

David Jeremiah
The Prayer Matrix (2004)

Prayer is the greatest power God has put into our hands for service— praying is harder work than doing, at least I find it so.

Mary Slessor
Mary Slessor of Calabar (1917)

Unless I had the spirit of prayer I could do nothing. If even for a day or an hour I lost the spirit of grace and supplication, I found myself unable to preach with power and efficiency, or to win souls by personal conversation.

Charles Finney
Memoirs of Rev. Charles G. Finney (1876)

The devil often laughs when we work, but he trembles when we pray.

Corrie ten Boom
Amazing Love (1953)

By praying more, we will not work any less, and we will accomplish vastly more.

R. A. Torrey
How to Bring Men to Christ (1893)

In your hour of desperation, where do you turn? Do you tell your troubles to anyone who will listen, or do you seek the throne of grace?

Michael Youssel
"A Prayer of Brokenness" (2009)

Prayer brings momentum. It lifts the heart above the challenges of life and gives it a view of God's resources of victory and hope.

John Mason
The Impossible Is Possible (2003)

Prayer may not change all things for you, but it sure changes you for all things.

John Mason
The Impossible Is Possible (2003)

More is accomplished by prayer than by anything else this world knows.

Ted Engstrom
Motivation to Last a Lifetime (1984)

Prayer is the preacher's mightiest weapon.

E. M. Bounds
Power Through Prayer (1906)

"In Everything by Prayer: An Unfailing Technique for Spiritual Success."

A. W. Tozer
sermon title (20th century)

For Christians prayer *is* like breathing. You don't have to think to breathe because the atmosphere exerts pressure on your lungs and forces you to breathe. That's why it is more difficult to hold your breath than it is to breathe. Similarly, when you're born into the family of God, you enter into a spiritual atmosphere wherein God's presence and grace exert pressure, or influence, on your life. Prayer is the normal response to that pressure.

John MacArthur
Alone with God (1995)

ANSWERED AND UNANSWERED PRAYER

Tho' dark the way, still trust and pray, the answering time will come.

Mary Wingate,
"The Answering Time Will Come" (1908)

God loves to hear and answer prayers. More often than not, He is the God of "Yes."

Dave Earley
The 21 Most Effective Prayers of the Bible (2005)

Be sure to remember that nothing in your daily life is so insignificant and so inconsequential that the Lord will not help you by answering your prayer.

O. Hallesby
Prayer (1931)

You thought God was to hear and answer you by making everything straight and pleasant—not so are nations or churches or men and women born; not so is character made. God is answering your prayer in His way.

Mary Slessor
Mary Slessor of Calabar (1917)

If we knock, God has promised to open the door and grant our request. It may be years before the answer comes; He may keep us knocking; but He has promised that the answer will come.

D. L. Moody
Prevailing Prayer: What Hinders It? (1884)

I ask Him daily and often momently to give me wisdom, understanding, and bodily strength to do His will; hence I am asking and receiving all the time.

George Washington Carver
George Washington Carver in His Own Words (1941)

We need to ask God to take this fragile, selfish, flawed self of ours and make it more like Him. God will answer that prayer.

Jerry Sittser
When God Doesn't Answer Your Prayer (2003)

I know what it is to pray long years and never get the answer—I had to pray for my father. But I know my heavenly Father so well I can leave it with Him for the lower fatherhood.

Mary Slessor
Mary Slessor of Calabar (1917)

Unanswered prayer never becomes a significant issue until we really need an answer to prayer, until our life depends on an answer. Then we cry out to God out of a deep sense of need. We pray out of desperation.

Jerry Sittser
When God Doesn't Answer Your Prayer (2003)

God detests the prayers of a man who has no delight in His Word. When we live with a closed Bible, we live with a closed heaven; God will not answer our prayers.

Charles Stanley
Handle with Prayer (1987)

No matter how intense or fervent or long your prayers may be, if you have unconfessed sin in your life, your prayers are really going nowhere.

Greg Laurie
Wrestling with God (2003)

The reason why we don't pray more—and probably don't see more answers to prayer—is not because we don't know how to pray but because we don't really need to pray. We are not desperate enough.

Jerry Sittser
When God Doesn't Answer Your Prayer (2003)

My life is one long daily, hourly record of answered prayer.

Mary Slessor
Mary Slessor of Calabar (1917)

We are to ask with a beggar's humility, to seek with a servant's carefulness, and to knock with the confidence of a friend.

D. L. Moody
Prevailing Prayer: What Hinders It? (1884)

Be specific with God in prayer, and He will be specific with you in regard to the answer.

David Wilkerson
Prayer—The Long and Short of It! (2009)

We must have a warrant for our prayers. If we have some great desire, we must search the scriptures to find if it be right to ask it.

D. L. Moody
Prevailing Prayer: What Hinders It? (1884)

We cannot be too frequent in our requests; God will not weary of His children's prayers.

D. L. Moody
Prevailing Prayer: What Hinders It? (1884)

There are more tears shed over answered prayers than over unanswered prayers.

Teresa of Avila
(16th century)

INTERCESSORY PRAYER

Have you ever learned the beautiful art of letting God take care of you and giving all your thought and strength to pray for others and for the kingdom of God? It will relieve you of a thousand cares.

A. B. Simpson
Days of Heaven Upon Earth (1897)

And that is the ultimate purpose of all this intercession: not just to save our own from the world, but to save the world through our own.

Agnes Sanford
The Healing Light (1947)

If we have our eyes and hearts open, there are many who need our prayers each day. Just reading the newspaper or watching the evening news provides ample opportunity for intercessory prayers—prayers on behalf of others.

Debra Farrington
A Beginner's Guide to Unceasing Prayer (2002)

When you pray for unconverted people, you do so on the assumption that it is in God's power to bring them to faith. You entreat Him to do that very thing, and your confidence in asking rests on the certainty that He is able to do what you ask.

J. I. Packer
Evangelism and the Sovereignty of God (2008)

When we hold up the life of another before God, when we expose it to God's love, when we pray. . .only then do we sense what it means to share in God's work, in His concern; only then do the walls that separate us from others go down and we sense that we are at bottom all knit together in a great and intimate family.

Douglas Steere
Prayer and Worship (1978)

There is no greater intimacy with another than that which is built through holding him or her up in prayer.

Douglas Steere
Prayer and Worship (1978)

Despite disappointments, the Christian is obligated to pray for the sick because we are bidden to do so and because the crumb of our caring is but a morsel broken from the whole loaf of the Father's infinite and tender love.

Catherine Marshall
Something More (1974)

Never stop praying for "hopeless" cases.

Robert Morgan
Moments for Families with Prodigals (2003)

Intercessory prayer is an extension of the ministry of Jesus through His Body, the Church, whereby we mediate between God and humanity for the purpose of reconciling the world to Him, or between Satan and humanity for the purpose of enforcing the victory of Calvary.

Dutch Sheets
Intercessory Prayer (1996)

There was a man convicted and converted in answer to prayer. So if you are anxious about the conversion of some relative, or some friend, make up your mind that you will give God no rest, day or night, till He grants your petition.

D. L. Moody
Prevailing Prayer: What Hinders It? (1884)

A "prayer warrior" is a person who is convinced that God is omnipotent—that God has the power to do anything, to change anyone, and to intervene in any circumstance. A person who truly believes this refuses to doubt God.

Bill Hybels
Too Busy Not to Pray (1988)

6
Some Prayers to Remember
SAMPLES OF FAMOUS PRAYERS
BY FAMOUS PEOPLE

PRAYERS OF DEVOTION TO GOD

My Lord God, I have no idea where I am going. I do not see the road ahead of me. I cannot know for certain where it will end. Nor do I really know myself, and the fact that I think I am following Your will does not mean that I am actually doing so. But I believe that the desire to please You does in fact please You. And I hope that I have that desire in all that I am doing. I hope that I will never do anything apart from that desire. And I know that if I do this You will lead me by the right road though I may know nothing about it. Therefore will I trust You always though I may seem to be lost and in the shadow of death. I will not fear, for You are ever with me, and will never leave me to face my perils alone.

Thomas Merton (1915–1968)

My God, I love Thee; not because
I hope for Heav'n thereby,
Nor yet because who love Thee not
May eternally die.

Thou, O my Jesus, Thou didst me
Upon the cross embrace;
For me didst bear the nails and spear,
And manifold disgrace.

And griefs and torments numberless,
And sweat of agony;
E'en death itself; and all for man
Who was Thine enemy.

Then why, O blessed Jesus Christ
Should I not love Thee well?
Not for the hope of winning heaven,
Nor of escaping hell.

Not with the hope of gaining aught,
Nor seeking a reward,
But as Thyself hast loved me,
O everlasting Lord!

E'en so I love Thee, and will love,
And in Thy praise will sing,
Solely because Thou art my God,
And my eternal King.

Attributed to Francis Xavier (1506–1552)

What shall I give You, Lord, in return for all Your kindness?
> Glory to You for Your love.
> Glory to You for Your mercy.
> Glory to You for Your patience.
> Glory to You for forgiving us all our sins.
> Glory to You for coming to save our souls.
> Glory to You for Your incarnation in the virgin's womb.
> Glory to You for Your bonds.
> Glory to You for receiving the cut of the lash.
> Glory to You for accepting mockery.
> Glory to You for Your crucifixion.
> Glory to You for Your burial.
> Glory to You for Your resurrection.
> Glory to You who as preached to men and women.
> Glory to You in whom they believed.
> Glory to You who was taken up into heaven.
> Glory to You who sits in the great glory at the Father's right hand.
> Glory to You whose will it is that the sinner should be saved through
> Your great mercy and compassion.

Ephraem of Syria (c. 306–373)

Thanks be to You, our Lord Jesus Christ, for all the benefits which You have given us, for all the pains and insults which You have borne for us. Most merciful Redeemer, Friend and Brother, may we know You more clearly, love You more dearly, and follow You more nearly, day by day.

Richard of Chichester (1197–1253)

Almighty God, in whom we live and move and have our being, who hast made us for Thyself, so that our hearts are restless till they rest in Thee: Grant us purity of heart and strength of purpose, that no selfish passion may hinder us from knowing Thy will, no weakness from doing it; but that in Thy light we may see light clearly, and in Thy service find our perfect freedom; through Jesus Christ our Lord.

Augustine of Hippo (345–430)

The Serenity Prayer

God grant me the serenity
To accept the things I cannot change;
Courage to change the things I can;
And wisdom to know the difference.
Living one day at a time;
Enjoying one moment at a time;
Accepting hardships as the pathway to peace;
Taking, as He did, this sinful world
As it is, not as I would have it;
Trusting that He will make all things right
If I surrender to His will;
So that I may be reasonably happy in this life
And supremely happy with Him
Forever and ever in the next.

Reinhold Niebuhr (1892–1971)

God of the day and of the night,
in me there is darkness,
but with You there is light.
I am alone, but You will not leave me.
I am weak, but You will come to my help.
I am restless, but You are my peace.
I am in haste, but You are the God
of infinite patience.
I am confused and lost,
but You are eternal wisdom
and You direct my path;
now and forever. Amen.

Dietrich Bonhoeffer (1906–1945)

St. Patrick's Breastplate

I arise today
Through a mighty strength,
the invocation of the Trinity,
Through the belief in the threeness,
Through confession of the oneness
Of the Creator of creation.

I arise today
Through the strength of Christ's birth
with His baptism,

Through the strength of His crucifixion with His burial,
Through the strength of His resurrection with His ascension,
Through the strength of His descent for the judgment of doom.
I arise today
Through the strength of the love of cherubim,
In obedience of angels,
In the service of archangels,
In hope of resurrection to meet with reward,
In prayers of patriarchs,
In predictions of prophets,
In preaching of apostles,
In faith of confessors,
In innocence of holy virgins,
In deeds of righteous men.

I arise today
Through the strength of heaven:
Light of sun,
Radiance of moon,
Splendor of fire,
Speed of lightning,
Swiftness of wind,
Depth of sea,
Stability of earth,
Firmness of rock.

I arise today
Through God's strength to pilot me,
God's might to uphold me,
God's wisdom to guide me,
God's eye to look before me,
God's ear to hear me,
God's word to speak for me,
God's hand to guard me,
God's way to lie before me,
God's shield to protect me,
God's host to save me
From snares of devils,
From temptations of vices,
From everyone who shall wish me ill,
Afar and anear,
Alone and in multitude.

I summon today all these powers between me and those evils,
Against every cruel merciless power
that may oppose my body and soul,
Against incantations of false prophets,
Against black laws of pagandom
Against false laws of heretics,
Against craft of idolatry,
Against spells of witches
and smiths and wizards,
Against every knowledge that corrupts
man's body and soul.
Christ to shield me today
Against poison, against burning,
Against drowning, against wounding,
So that there may come to me
abundance of reward.

Christ with me, Christ before me,
Christ behind me,
Christ in me, Christ beneath me,
Christ above me,
Christ on my right, Christ on my left,
Christ when I lie down, Christ when I sit down,
Christ when I arise,
Christ in the heart of every man
who thinks of me,
Christ in the mouth of everyone
who speaks of me,
Christ in every eye that sees me,
Christ in every ear that hears me.

I arise today
Through a mighty strength, the invocation of the Trinity,
Through belief in the threeness,
Through confession of the oneness,
Of the Creator of creation.

St. Patrick of Ireland (387–493)

O Lord, teach me to seek You, and reveal Yourself to me when I seek You. For
I cannot seek You unless You first teach me, nor find You unless You first reveal
Yourself to me. Let me seek You in longing, and long for You in seeking. Let me
find You in love, and love You in finding.

Ambrose of Milan (c. 340–397)

O Lord, who in infinite wisdom and love orders all things for Your children, order everything this day for me in Your tender pity. You know my weakness, who made me; You know how my soul shrinks from all pain of soul. Lord, I know You will lay no greater burden on me than You can help me to bear. Teach me to receive all things this day from You. Enable me to commend myself in all things to You; grant me in all things to please You; bring me through all things nearer to You; bring me, day by day, nearer to Yourself, to life everlasting. Amen.

Edward Bouverie Pusey (1800–1882)

PRAYERS OF COMMITMENT TO SERVICE

Prayer of St. Francis
Lord, make me an instrument of Your peace;
where there is hatred, let me sow love;
where there is injury, pardon;
where there is doubt, faith;
where there is despair, hope;
where there is darkness, light;
and where there is sadness, joy.

O divine Master,
grant that I may not so much seek to be consoled as to console;
to be understood, as to understand;
to be loved, as to love;
for it is in giving that we receive,
it is in pardoning that we are pardoned,
and it is in dying that we are born to eternal life.

Francis of Assisi (1181–1226)

Strengthen us, our God, to relieve the oppressed, to hear the groans of poor prisoners, to reform the abuses from all professionals, that many be made not poor to make a few rich.

Oliver Cromwell (1599–1658)

God of love, we pray that You give us love: love in our thinking, love in our speaking, love in our doing, and love in the hidden places of our souls; love of our neighbors, near and far; love of our friends, old and new; love of those whom we find it hard to bear, and love of those who find it hard to bear with us; love of those with whom we work, and love of those with whom we take our ease; love in joy, love in sorrow; love in life and love in death; that so at length we may be worthy to dwell with You, who are eternal love, Father, Son, and Holy Spirit, forever and ever.

William Temple (1881–1944)

Lord when I am hungry,
give me someone needing food;
When I am thirsty,
send me someone needing a drink;
When I am cold, send me
someone to warm;
When I am grieved, send me
someone to console;
When my cross grows heavy
let me carry another's cross, too;
When I am poor, lend me
someone in need;
When I have no time,
give me someone I can help a little while;
When I am humiliated,
let me have someone to praise;
When I am disheartened,
send me someone to cheer;
When I need understanding,
give me someone who needs mine;
When I need to be looked after,
give me someone to care for;
When I think only of myself,
draw my thoughts to another.

Author Unknown

Lord, give us such a strong love for You as may sweeten our obedience. Let us not serve You with the spirit of bondage as slaves, but with cheerfulness and gladness, rejoicing in Your work.

Benjamin Jenks (1646–1724)

Teach us, good Lord, to serve You
as You deserve:
to give, and not to count the cost,
to fight, and not to heed the wounds,
to toil, and not to seek for rest,
to labor, and not to ask for any reward,
save that of knowing that we do Your will.

Ignatius of Loyola (1491–1556)

Dear Jesus, help us to spread your fragrance everywhere we go; flood our souls with Your Spirit and life. Penetrate and possess our whole being so utterly that our lives may only be a radiance of Yours. Shine through us and be so in us that every soul we come in contact with may feel Your presence in our soul. Let them look up and see no longer us but only Jesus. Stay with us and then we shall begin to shine as You shine, so to shine as to be light to others. The light, O Jesus, will be all from You. None of it will be ours. It will be Your shining on others through us. Let us thus praise You in the way You love best by shining on those around us. Let us preach You without preaching, not by words, but by our example, by the catching force the sympathetic influence of what we do, the evident fullness of the love our hearts bear to You.

Mother Teresa of Calcutta (1910–1997)

Lord, open my eyes that I may see the needs of others, open my ears that I may hear their cries, open my heart so that they need not be without relief. Let me not be afraid to defend the weak because of the anger of the strong, nor afraid to defend the poor because of the anger of the rich. Show me where love and hope and faith are needed, and use me to bring them to these places. Open my eyes and ears that I may, this coming day, be able to do some work of peace for You.

Alan Stewart Paton (1903–1988)

Use me, then, my Savior, for whatever purpose and in whatever way You may require. Here is my poor heart, an empty vessel. Fill it with Your grace.

D. L. Moody (1837–1899)

Lord Jesus, bless all who serve us, who have dedicated their lives to the ministry of others—all the teachers of our schools who labor so patiently with so little appreciation; all who wait upon the public, the clerks in the stores who have to accept criticism, complaints, bad manners, and selfishness at the hands of a thoughtless public. Bless the mailman, the drivers of streetcars and buses who must listen to people who lose their tempers. Bless every humble soul who, in these days of stress and strain, preaches sermons without words. Amen.

Peter Marshall (1902–1949)

Make us worthy, Lord, to serve our fellow men throughout the world who live and die in poverty and hunger. Give them, through our hands, this day their daily bread, and by our understanding love, give peace and joy.

Mother Teresa of Calcutta (1910–1997)

Let us go forth
In the goodness of our merciful Father,
In the gentleness of our brother Jesus,
In the radiance of His Holy Spirit,
In the faith of the apostles,
In the joyful praise of the angels,
In the holiness of the saints,
In the courage of the martyrs.

Celtic Prayer

Hands who touched the leper, touch my wounded heart;
Hands who healed the blind man, heal my aching soul;
Hands who cured the lame, mend my disjointed life;
Hands who embraced all life, enfold me in Your peace.
Lord, merely touch and heal, cure and forgive.

This is my prayer to Thee, my Lord;
Give me strength lightly to bear my joys and sorrows;
Give me the strength to make my love fruitful in service;
Give me the strength never to disown the poor
or bend my knees before insolent might.
Give me the strength to raise my mind high above daily trifles.
And give me the strength to surrender my strength
to Thy will with love.

Rabindranath Tagore (1861–1941)

O Lord, give us more charity, more self-denial, more likeness to You. Teach us to sacrifice our comforts to others, and our likings for the sake of doing good. Make us kindly in thought, gentle in word, generous in deed. Teach us that it is better to give than to receive, better to forget ourselves than to put ourselves forward, better to minister than to be ministered unto. And to You, God of love, be all glory and praise, now and forever. Amen.

Henry Alford (1810–1871)

Lord, baptize our hearts into a sense of the needs and conditions of all.

George Fox (1624–1691)

Prayers for Times of Adversity/Suffering

Give me my scallop shell of quiet,
My staff of faith to walk upon,
My scrip of joy, immortal diet,
My bottle of salvation,

My gown of glory, hope's true gage,
And thus I'll take my pilgrimage.

Sir Walter Raleigh (1552–1618),
just before his execution

THE BLESSING OF UNANSWERED PRAYERS

I asked for strength that I might achieve;
I was made weak that I might
learn humbly to obey.
I asked for health that I might do greater things;
I was given infirmity that I might do better things.
I asked for riches that I might be happy;
I was given poverty that I might be wise.
I asked for power that I might have the praise of men;
I was given weakness that I might feel the need of God.
I asked for all things that I might enjoy life;
I was given life that I might enjoy all things.
I got nothing that I had asked for,
but everything that I had hoped for.
Almost despite myself my unspoken prayers were answered;
I am, among all men, most richly blessed.

Unknown Confederate Soldier

Grant that for Your sake I may come to love and desire any hardship that
puts me to the test, for salvation is brought to my soul when I undergo
suffering and trouble for You.

Thomas à Kempis (1380–1471)

THE ALPHABET PRAYER

Although things are not perfect,
Because of trial or pain,
Continue in thanksgiving
Do not begin to blame;
Even when the times are hard,
Fierce winds are bound to blow,
God is forever able;
Hold on to what you know.
Imagine life without His love
Joy would cease to be,
Keep thanking Him for all the things
Love imparts to thee.

Move out of "Camp Complaining,"
No weapon that is known
On earth can yield the power
Praise can do alone.
Quit looking at the future,
Redeem the time at hand;
Start every day with worship,
To "thank" is a command.
Until we see Him coming
Victorious in the sky,
We'll run the race with gratitude
Xalting God most high.
Yes, there'll be good times
and yes, some will be bad,
but. . .Zion waits in glory. . .
Where none are ever sad!

Author Unknown

Help us to bear difficulty, pain, disappointment, and sorrows, knowing that in Your perfect working and design, You can use such bitter experiences to shape our character and make us more like our Lord.

Ignatius of Antioch (c. 30–107),
before his martyrdom

Lord God Almighty, the Father of Your well-beloved and blessed Son, Jesus Christ, by whom we have received knowledge of You, the God of angels and powers, and of every creature, and especially the whole race of just men who live in Your presence: I give thee hearty thanks that You have thought me worthy of this day and hours, to be numbered among Your martyrs, and to share in the cup of Christ, for resurrection to eternal life, for soul and body, in the incorruptibility of the Holy Spirit. Among them may I be accepted before You today, as a rich and acceptable sacrifice, just as You, the faithful and true God, have both ordained and prepared this day and also have now fulfilled it. For this reason, and for everything else, I praise You, bless You, and glorify You by the eternal and heavenly high priest, Jesus Christ, Your beloved Son, through whom be glory to You, with Him and the Holy Spirit, now and for the ages to come. Amen.

Polycarp (69–155),
as he awaited execution at the stake

Comfort, merciful Father, by Your word and the Holy Spirit, all who are afflicted or distressed, and so turn their hearts to You, that they may serve You in truth and bring forth fruit for Your glory.

Philip Melanchthon (1467–1560)

PRAYERS OF REPENTANCE/CONFESSION

O Lord, give us all, we beseech Thee, grace and strength to overcome every sin; sins of besetment, deliberation, surprise, negligence, omission; sins against Thee, ourself, our neighbor; sins great, small, remembered, forgotten. Amen.

Christina Rossetti (1830–1895)

Almighty God, Father of mercies, be pleased to work in me what Thou hast commended should be in me. Give me, O Lord, the grace of an earnest sorrow—turn my sin into repentance, and let my repentance proceed to pardon; and teach me so diligently to watch over all my actions that I may never transgress Thy holy laws willingly, but that it may be the work of my life to obey Thee, the joy of my soul to please Thee, and the perfection of my desires to live with Thee in the kingdom of Thy grace and glory. Amen.

Jeremy Taylor (1613–1667)

O Lord, my God, light of the blind and strength of the weak; yea, also, light of those that see, and strength of the strong; hearken unto my soul, and hear it crying out of the depths.

O Lord, help us to turn and seek Thee; for Thou hast not forsaken Thy creatures as we have forsaken Thee, our Creator. Let us turn and seek Thee, for we know Thou art here in our hearts, when we confess to Thee, when we cast ourselves upon Thee, and weep in Thy bosom, after all our rugged ways; and Thou dost gently wipe away our tears, and we weep the more for joy; because Thou, Lord, who madest us, dost remake and comfort us.

Hear, Lord, my prayer, and grant that I may most entirely love Thee, and do Thou rescue me, O Lord, from every temptation, even unto the end. Amen.

Augustine of Hippo (345–430)

O searcher of hearts, Thou knowest us better than we know ourselves, and seest the sins which our sinfulness hides from us. Yet even our own conscience beareth witness against us, that we often slumber on our appointed watch; that we walk not always lovingly with each other and humbly with Thee; and we withhold that entire sacrifice of ourselves to Thy perfect will, without which we are not crucified with Christ, or sharers in His redemption. Oh look upon our contrition and lift up our weakness, and let the dayspring yet arise within our hearts, and bring us healing, strength, and joy. Day by day may we grow in faith, in self-denial, in charity, in heavenly-mindedness. And then, mingle us at last with the mighty host of Thy redeemed forevermore. Amen.

James Martineau (1805–1900)

O merciful God, full of compassion, long-suffering and of great pity, make me earnestly repent and heartily to be sorry for all my misdoings; make the remembrance of them so burdensome and painful that I may flee to Thee with a troubled spirit and a contrite heart; and, O merciful Lord, visit, comfort, and relieve me; excite in me true repentance; give me in this world knowledge of Thy truth and confidence in Thy mercy, and, in the world to come, life everlasting. Strengthen me against sin, and enable so to perform every duty, that whilst I live I may serve Thee in that state to which Thou hast called me; and, at last, by a holy and happy death, be delivered from the struggles and sorrows of this life and obtain eternal happiness, for the sake of our Lord and Savior, Thy Son Jesus Christ. Amen.

Samuel Johnson (1709–1784)

O Thou gracious and gentle and condescending God, Thou God of peace, Father of mercy, God of all comfort; see, I lament before Thee the evil of my heart; I acknowledge that I am too much disposed to anger, jealousy, and revenge, to ambition and pride, which often give rise to discord and bitter feelings between me and others. Too often have I thus offended and grieved both Thee, O long-suffering Father, and my fellow men. Oh forgive me this sin, and suffer me to partake of the blessing which Thou hast promised to the peacemakers, who shall be called the children of God. Bestow on me, O Lord, a genial spirit and unwearied forbearance; a mild, loving, patient heart; kindly looks, pleasant, cordial speech and manners in the intercourse of daily life; that I may give offence to none, but as much as in me lies live in charity with all men. Amen.

Johann Arndt (1555–1621)

I offer up unto Thee my prayers and intercessions for those especially who have in any matter hurt, grieved, or found fault with me, or who have done me any damage or displeasure.

For all those also whom, at any time, I may have vexed, troubled, burdened, and scandalized, by words or deeds, knowingly or in ignorance; that Thou wouldst grant us all equally pardon for our sins, and for our offences against each other. Take away from our hearts, O Lord, all suspiciousness, indignation, wrath, and contention, and whatsoever may hurt charity and lessen brotherly love. Have mercy, O Lord, have mercy on those that crave Thy mercy; give grace unto them that stand in need thereof, and make us such as that we may be worthy to enjoy Thy grace and go forward to life eternal. Amen.

Thomas à Kempis (c. 1380–1471)

O Thou, who knowest our hearts, and who seest our temptations and struggles, have pity upon us, and deliver us from the sins which make war upon our souls. Thou art all-powerful and we are weak and erring. Our trust is in Thee, O Thou faithful and good God. Deliver us from the bondage of evil, and grant that we may thereafter be Thy devoted servants, serving Thee in the freedom of holy love, for Christ's sake. Amen.

Eugène Bersier (1830–1903)

O sweet Savior Christ, in Your undeserved love for us You were prepared to suffer the painful death of the cross: let me not be cold or even lukewarm in my love for You. Lord, help me to face the truth about myself. Help me to hear my words as others hear them, to see my face as others see me; let me be honest enough to recognize my impatience and conceit; let me recognize my anger and selfishness; give me sufficient humility to accept my own weaknesses for what they are. Give me the grace—at least in Your presence—to say, "I was wrong—forgive me." God, the Father of our Lord Jesus Christ, increase in us faith and truth and gentleness and grant us part and lot among the saints.

Polycarp (69–155)

Dear Lord and Father of Mankind (Abridged)

> Dear Lord and Father of mankind,
> Forgive our foolish ways!
> Reclothe us in our rightful mind,
> In purer lives Thy service find,
> In deeper reverence, praise.
> Drop Thy still dews of quietness,
> Till all our strivings cease;
> Take from our souls the strain and stress,
> And let our ordered lives confess
> The beauty of Thy peace.

Breathe through the heat of our desire
Thy coolness and Thy balm;
Let sense be dumb, let flesh retire;
Speak through the earthquake, wind, and fire,
O still, small voice of calm!

John Greenleaf Whittier (1807–1892)

Most merciful Father, we come before Your throne in the name of Jesus Christ, that for His sake alone You will have compassion on us, and not let our sins be a cloud between You and us.

John Colet (1467(?)–1519)

Forgive them all, O Lord; our sins of omission and our sins of commission; the sins of our youth and the sins of our riper years; the sins of our souls and the sins of our bodies; our secret and our more open sins; our sins of ignorance and surprise, and our more deliberate and presumptuous sin; the sins we have done to please ourselves, and the sins we have done to please others; the sins we know and remember and the sins we have forgotten; the sins we have striven to hide from others and the sins by which we have made others offend. Forgive them, O Lord, forgive them all for His sake, who died for our sins and rose for our justification and now stands at Thy right hand to make intercession for us, Jesus Christ our Lord.

John Wesley (1662–1735)

Almighty, forgive my doubt, my anger, my pride. By Your mercy abase me, in Your strictness raise me up.

Dag Hammarskjöld (1905–1961)

7

Not Your "Everyday" Prayers
PRAYERS FOR HOLIDAYS/SPECIAL OCCASIONS

CHRISTMAS PRAYERS

Loving Father, help us remember the birth of Jesus, that we may share in the song of the angels, the gladness of the shepherds, and worship of the wise men.

Close the door of hate and open the door of love all over the world. Let kindness come with every gift and good desires with every greeting. Deliver us from evil by the blessing which Christ brings, and teach us to be merry with clear hearts.

May the Christmas morning make us happy to be Thy children, and Christmas evening bring us to our beds with grateful thoughts, forgiving and forgiven, for Jesus' sake. Amen.

Robert Louis Stevenson (1850–1894)

We yearn, our Father, for the simple beauty of Christmas—for all the old familiar melodies and words that remind us of that great miracle when He who had made all things was one night to come as a babe, to lie in the crook of a woman's arm.

Before such mystery we kneel, as we follow the shepherds and wise men to bring Thee the gift of our love—a love we confess has not always been as warm or sincere or real as it should have been. But now, on this Christmas Day, that love would find its Beloved, and from Thee receive the grace to make it pure again, warm and real.

We bring Thee our gratitude for every token of Thy love, for all the ways Thou hast heaped blessings upon us during the years that have gone.

And we do pray, Lord Jesus, that as we celebrate Thy birthday, we may do it in a manner well pleasing to Thee. May all we do and say, every tribute of our hearts, bring honor to Thy name, that we, Thy people, may remember Thy birth and feel Thy presence among us even yet.

May the loving-kindness of Christmas not only creep into our hearts, but there abide, so that not even the return to earthly cares and responsibilities, not all the festivities of our own devising may cause it to creep away weeping. May the joy and spirit of Christmas stay with us now and forever.

In the name of Jesus, who came to save His people from their sins, even in that lovely name we pray. Amen.

Peter Marshall (1902–1942)

Moonless darkness stands between.
Past, the past, no more be seen!
But the Bethlehem star may lead me
To the sight of Him who freed me
From the self that I have been.
Make me pure, Lord: Thou art holy;
Make me meek, Lord: Thou wert lowly;
Now beginning, and alway:
Now begin, on Christmas Day.

Gerard Manley Hopkins (1844–1889)

Good Jesus, born at this time, a little child of love for us: be born in me so
that I may be a little child in love with You.

Edward Bouverie Pusey (1800–1882)

As on this day we keep the special memory of our Redeemer's entry into the
city, so grand, Lord, that now and ever he may triumph in our hearts. Let
the king of grace and glory enter in, and let us lay ourselves and all we are
in the full joyful homage before him.

H. C. G. Moule (1841–1920)

Ah, dearest Jesus, holy child,
Make thee a bed, soft, undefiled,
Within my heart, that it may be
A quiet chamber kept for Thee.

My heart for very joy doth leap,
My lips no more can silence keep,
I, too, must sing, with joyful tongue,
That sweetest ancient song,

Glory to God in highest heaven,
Who unto man His Son hath given
While angels sing with pious mirth.
A glad new year to all the earth!

Martin Luther (1483–1546)

How silently, how silently,
the wondrous Gift is giv'n;
So God imparts to human hearts
the blessings of His heav'n.
No ear may hear His coming,
but in this world of sin,
Where meek souls will receive Him still,
the dear Christ enters in.

O holy child of Bethlehem,
descend to us, we pray;
Cast out our sin, and enter in,
be born in us today.
We hear the Christmas angels
the great glad tidings tell;
O come to us, abide with us,
our Lord Emmanuel!

Philips Brooks (1835–1893),
from "O Little Town of Bethlehem"

Let Your goodness, Lord, appear to us, that we made in Your image, conform ourselves to it. In our own strength we cannot imitate Your majesty, power, and wonder; nor is it fitting for us to try. But Your mercy reaches from the heavens through the clouds to the earth below. You have come to us as a small child, but you have brought us the greatest of all gifts, the gift of eternal love; caress us with Your tiny hands, embrace us with Your tiny arms and pierce our hearts with Your soft, sweet cries.

Bernard of Clairvaux (1090–1153)

Loving God, we give thanks for the birth of Your Son Jesus Christ, both in human form in Bethlehem and in spiritual form in our hearts. May He reign as king within every human heart, so that every town and village can live according to His joyful law of love.

Thomas Münzer (1490–1525)

GOOD FRIDAY

Good Friday in My Heart

Good Friday in my heart! Fear and affright!
My thoughts are the disciples when they fled,
My words the words that priest and soldier said,
My deed the spear to desecrate the dead.
And day, Thy death therein, is changed to night.

Then Easter in my heart sends up the sun.
My thoughts are Mary, when she turned to see.
My words are Peter, answering, 'Lov'st thou Me?'
My deeds are all Thine own drawn close to Thee,
And night and day, since Thou dost rise, are one.

Mary Elizabeth Coleridge (1861–1907)

Jesus, You let your side be opened by the spear so that there could come forth blood and water; wound my heart with the spear of charity so that I may be made worthy of Your sacraments which flow from Your most holy side.

Ludolf of Saxony (c. 1300–c. 1378)

Almighty and eternal God, merciful Father, who has given to the human race Your beloved Son as an example of humility, obedience, and patience, to precede us on the way of life, bearing the cross: graciously grant that we be inflamed by His infinite love so that way may take up the sweet yoke of His gospel, following Him as His true disciples, so that we shall one day gloriously rise with Him and joyfully hear the final sentence: "Come, you blessed of My Father, and possess the kingdom which was prepared for you from the beginning," where You reign with the Son and the Holy Ghost, and where we hope to reign with You, world without end.

Francis of Assisi (1181–1226)

Grant, Lord, that in Your wounds I may find my safety, in Your stripes my cure, in Your pain my peace, in Your cross my victory, in Your resurrection my triumph.

Jeremy Taylor (1613–1667)

EASTER (RESURRECTION DAY)

It is only right, with all the powers of our heart and mind, to praise You, Father, and Your only begotten Son, our Lord Jesus Christ: dear Father, by Your wondrous condescension of loving-kindness toward us, Your servants, You gave up Your Son.

Dear Jesus, You paid the debt of Adam for us to the eternal Father by Your blood poured forth in loving-kindness. You cleared away the darkness of sin by Your magnificent and radiant resurrection. You broke the bonds of death and rose from the grave as a conqueror.

You reconciled heaven and earth. Our life had no hope of eternal happiness before You redeemed us. Your resurrection has washed away our sins, restored our innocence, and brought us joy.

How inestimable is the tenderness of Your love!

Gregory the Great (540–604)

O God, who for our redemption gave Your only begotten Son to the death of the cross, and by His glorious resurrection delivered us from the power of our enemy: grant us so to die daily to sin, that we may evermore live with Him in the joy of His resurrection.

Anglican Easter Prayer

I see flames of orange, yellow, and red shooting upward to the sky, piercing the whole clouds. I see the clouds themselves chasing the flames upward, and I feel the air itself reaching for the heavens.

Down below I see great, gray rocks beating against the earth, as if they were pushing their way down to hell.

At Your resurrection, that which is light and good rises up with You, and that which is heavy and evil is pushed downward.

At Your resurrection, goodness breaks from evil, life breaks free from death.

The Victorines

Almighty God, who through the death of Your Son has destroyed sin and death and by His resurrection has restored the innocence and everlasting life so we could be saved from the power of the devil, and so our mortal bodies raised up from the dead: grant that we may confidently and wholeheartedly believe this message and that, finally, we may share with Your saints in the joyful resurrection of those who have been justified through You.

Martin Luther (1483–1546)

BIRTHDAYS

Almighty and everlasting God, the maker of all creation: mercifully hear our prayer and grant many and happy years to Your servant whose birthday it is, that he may spend all his life so as to please You, through Jesus Christ our Lord.

The Gelasian Sacramentary (8th Century)

Eternal Father, the giver of life, who on this day caused Your servant to be born into this world: we thank You, Lord, for all Your mercies granted to him from that time until now and humbly ask You to continue Your gracious favor and protection until his life's end. Help him in every time of trial, shield him in danger, relieve and comfort him in trouble, assist him against temptation, defend him from the assaults of the enemy, so that his days here may pass in peace so that when he dies, he may attain unto the everlasting rest that remains for Your people.

William Edward Scudamore (1813–1881)

BAPTISM

Look down from heaven, Lord, upon Your flock and Your lambs. Bless their bodies and their souls, and grant that those who have received the sign of the cross on their foreheads at baptism may be shown to belong to You on the day of judgment, through Jesus Christ our Lord.

Egbert of York (d. 766)

Make Yourself manifest, Lord, in this water, and grant to him who is baptized in it so to be transformed that he may put off the old man, which is corrupted by deceitful lusts, and may put on the new man, which is formed fresh according to the image of the Creator. Grafted through baptism into the likeness of Your death, may he become a partaker also in Your resurrection. May he guard the gift of Your Holy Spirit, may he increase in the measure of grace, which has been entrusted to him, and may he receive the prize which is God's calling to life above, being numbered among the firstborn whose names are written in heaven.

Eastern Orthodox Baptismal

Almighty and eternal God, most merciful Father, as the just live by faith and as it is impossible for anyone to please You without faith, we pray that You will grant to this child the gift of faith, in which You will seal and assure his heart in the Holy Spirit, according to the promise of Your Son; that the inner regeneration of the Spirit may be truly represented by the outward baptism, and that the child may be buried with Christ into death and be raised up from death by Christ, to the praise of Your glory and the building up of his neighbor.

Miles Coverdale (1488–1568)

Lord of the flood, wash us with Your Spirit that we may be Your ark of life, Your peace in the sea of violence. Water is life; water cleans; water kills. Frightened, we are tempted to make a permanent home on the ark. But You force us to seek dry ground. We can do so only because You have taught us to cling to our baptisms, when we are drowned and reborn by the water and fire of Your Spirit. So reborn, make us unafraid. Amen.

Stanley Hauerwas (b. 1940)

WEDDINGS/MARRIAGE

Wedding Blessing

God, the best maker of all marriages,
combine your hearts in one,
your realms in one.

William Shakespeare (1564–1616)

Blessed be the light that has guided your souls to the threshold of this new day.

Blessed be the journey you walk as one sharing your love with the world.

Blessed be the stillness that refreshes your souls and awakens God's dream in your hearts. The shield of the God of life be yours.

The compassion of the loving Christ be yours.

The wisdom of the living Spirit be yours.

Now and evermore.

Celtic Christian Wedding Blessing

Most gracious God, we give You thanks for Your tender love in sending Jesus Christ to come among us, to be born of a human mother, and to make the way of the cross to be the way of life. We thank You, also, for consecrating the union of man and woman in His name.

By the power of Your Holy Spirit, pour out the abundance of Your blessing upon this man and this woman. Defend them from every enemy. Lead them into all peace. Let their love for each other be a seal upon their hearts, a mantle about their shoulders, and a crown upon their foreheads. Bless them in their work and in their companionship; in their sleeping and in their waking; in their joys and in their sorrows; in their life and in their death.

Finally, in Your mercy, bring them to that table where Your saints feast forever in Your heavenly home; through Jesus Christ our Lord, who with You and the Holy Spirit lives and reigns, one God, forever and ever. Amen.

Book of Common Prayer

Lord, help us to remember when we first met and the strong love that grew between us.

To work that love into practical things so nothing can divide us. We ask for words both kind and loving and for hearts always ready to ask forgiveness as well as to forgive. Dear Lord, we put our marriage into Your hands. Amen.

Author Unknown

WEDDING PRAYER

Lord, behold our family here assembled.

We thank You for this place in which we dwell,

for the love that unites us,

for the peace accorded us this day,

for the hope with which we expect the morrow,

for the health, the work, the food,

and the bright skies that make our lives delightful;

for our friends in all parts of the earth.

Amen.

Robert Louis Stevenson (1850–1894)

BEREAVEMENT/FUNERALS

Catholic Funeral Prayer

God our Father,
Your power brings us to birth,
Your providence guides our lives,
and by Your command we return to dust.
Lord, those who die still live in Your presence,
their lives change but do not end.
I pray in hope for my family,
relatives, and friends,
and for all the dead known to You alone.
In company with Christ,
Who died and now lives,
may they rejoice in Your kingdom,
where all our tears are wiped away.
Unite us together again in one family,
to sing Your praise forever and ever.
Amen.

Ah, poor lonely widow and miserable woman that I am, may He who does not forsake widows and orphans console me. O my God, console me! O my Jesus, strengthen me in my weakness!

Elizabeth of Hungary (1207–1231),
after the death of her husband

If Death My Friend and Me Divide

If death my friend and me divide,
Thou dost not, Lord, my sorrow chide,
Or frown my tears to see;
Restrained from passionate excess,
Thou bidst me mourn in calm distress
For them that rest in Thee.

I feel a strong immortal hope,
Which bears my mournful spirit up
Beneath its mountain load;
Redeemed from death, and grief, and pain,
I soon shall find my friend again

Within the arms of God.
Pass a few fleeting moments more
And death the blessing shall restore

Which death has snatched away;
For me Thou wilt the summons send,
And give me back my parted friend
In that eternal day.

Charles Wesley (1707–1788)

O God, to me who am left to mourn his departure, grant that I may not sorrow as one without hope for my beloved who sleeps in You; but as always remembering his courage and the love that united us on earth, I may begin again with new courage to serve You more fervently who are the only source of true love and true fortitude that when I have passed a few more days in this valley of tears and this shadow of death, supported by Your rod and staff, I may see him face to face, in those pastures and beside those waters of comfort where I believe he already walks with You. O Shepherd of the sheep, have pity on this darkened soul of mine.

Edward White Benson (1829–1896),
after the death of his young son

God of all consolation, in Your unending love and mercy for us, You turn the darkness of death into the dawn of new life.

Show compassion to Your people in their sorrow, be our refuge and our strength, to lift us from the darkness of this grief to the peace and light of Your presence.

Your Son, our Lord Jesus Christ, by dying for us, conquered death, and by rising again, restored to us eternal life: may we then go forward eagerly to meet our Redeemer and, after our life on earth, be reunited with all our brothers and sisters in that place where every tear is wiped away and all things are made new, through Jesus Christ our Savior.

The Roman Catholic *Family Prayer Book*

It Is Well with My Soul

When peace, like a river, attendeth my way,
When sorrows like sea billows roll;
Whatever my lot, Thou has taught me to say,
It is well, it is well, with my soul.

It is well, with my soul,
It is well, with my soul,
It is well, it is well, with my soul.
Though Satan should buffet,
though trials should come,
Let this blest assurance control,

That Christ has regarded my helpless estate,
And hath shed His own blood for my soul.

It is well, with my soul,
It is well, with my soul,
It is well, it is well, with my soul.

My sin, oh, the bliss of this glorious thought!
My sin, not in part but the whole,
Is nailed to the cross, and I bear it no more,
Praise the Lord, praise the Lord, O my soul!

It is well, with my soul,
It is well, with my soul,
It is well, it is well, with my soul.

And Lord, haste the day when
my faith shall be sight,
The clouds be rolled back as a scroll;
The trump shall resound, and the Lord shall descend,
Even so, it is well with my soul.

It is well, with my soul,
It is well, with my soul,
It is well, it is well, with my soul.

Horatio G. Spafford (1828–1888),
after the tragic death of his four daughters

PRAYERS &
promises

Toni Sortor
Pamela L. McQuade
John Hudson Tiner

PREFACE

God's promises have richly blessed Christians through the ages. They have offered solutions to problems, strength during trials, and inspiration for the Christian life.

In these pages, we provide nearly ninety prayers based on many of Scripture's promises. Whether you are struggling with guilt or fear or need to draw close to God's loving heart, grab hold of a truth in Scripture and share a heartfelt prayer.

Pray, and experience the truth of God's promise to Jeremiah: "Call unto me, and I will answer thee, and show thee great and mighty things, which thou knowest not" (Jeremiah 33:3).

ATTITUDE

Create in me a clean heart, O God;
and renew a right spirit within me.

PSALM 51:10

Father, I am quick to focus on those things that affect me most directly. Often, I confess, I improperly view my wants as essentials. From minor matters such as restaurant service to more important ones such as making major purchases, I insist that my so-called requirements be fully met. I think and act as if those serving me should put my needs first.

Lord, keep a check on my attitude. I want to have a friendly disposition when I deal with others. Create in me a calm, controlled temperament. Help me have a "can do," "everything's okay" attitude rather than a "me" attitude.

MY PRAYERS

_____

_____

_____

_____

_____

AVOIDING DOUBT

Jesus replied, "I tell you the truth,
if you have faith and do not doubt,
not only can you do what was done to the fig tree,
but also you can say to this mountain,
'Go, throw yourself into the sea,'
and it will be done."

MATTHEW 21:21 NIV

It's hard for me to imagine this kind of faith, Lord. So often my own seems to get stuck under mountains instead of moving them. But I know that if You promise such things, they can happen.

Remove my doubt, O Lord. As I trust more fully in You, I know my faith will become strong enough to do Your will. That may not include mountain moving, but I know it can change lives, bring hope, and draw others to You.

Actually, you might call that moving a mountain, after all!

MY PRAYERS

_____

_____

_____

_____

_____

THE BEAUTY
OF HOLINESS

Give unto the LORD the glory due unto his name:
bring an offering, and come before him:
worship the LORD in the beauty of holiness.

1 CHRONICLES 16:29

Holiness is true beauty, not what I wear or how my hair is done or how white my teeth shine. Indeed, holiness is Yours, never mine. I am fatally flawed, but I worship One who is perfect in all ways, One whose glory alone is worthy of praise and thanksgiving. There is no beauty compared to Yours, no faithfulness like Yours. The little glimpses of beauty that decorate my life are grains of silver sand at the edge of an incomprehensible ocean of beauty. I only see a grain or two in my lifetime, but it dazzles my eyes and makes me turn away blinking. I worship You in the beauty of Your holiness.

MY PRAYERS

_____

_____

_____

_____

_____

BELIEVING
WITHOUT SEEING

Whom having not seen, ye love;
in whom, though now ye see him not,
yet believing, ye rejoice with
joy unspeakable and full of glory:
Receiving the end of your faith,
even the salvation of your souls.

1 PETER 1:8–9

I am one of Your peculiar people, Lord, set apart from the world by both my beliefs and my actions. I have never seen even Your sandal prints at the edge of the lake, yet I follow You with all my heart. My ears have never heard Your voice, but I live by Your words. My fingertips have never brushed the edge of Your garment, yet I am healed. My belief is not based in my senses or my intellect but in Your never failing love, which saved my soul and promises me unspeakable joy.

MY PRAYERS

_____

_____

_____

_____

_____

A BROKEN SPIRIT

A merry heart doeth good like a medicine:
but a broken spirit drieth the bones.

PROVERBS 17:22

If a broken spirit dries the bones, Lord, about now mine should be dust. I'm not at all content with my situation, and my heart is down in the dumps. Turn my spirit toward You again, where I can find the joy and contentment I'm missing. May I feel Your Spirit touch my heart so that I may bring good to those I see each day. Help me rejoice in You, no matter what is going on in my life. I don't want sin to turn me into a pile of dry bones, and I don't want to share that attitude with others. Pour Your blessed balm on my aching heart, O Lord.

MY PRAYERS

_____

_____

_____

_____

_____

THE COMPANY OF SINNERS

For I am not come to call the righteous,
but sinners to repentance.

MATTHEW 9:13

Father, examine the way I use my time in Your service. Am I too comfortable? Do I spend my time in fellowship with other believers because it is pleasant and safe, or do I risk the company of sinners? Who needs me most, my neighbor in the pew or my brother and sister in need of repentance and forgiveness? How can I be more effective in my outreach and missionary work?

Your Son showed me by example how I should be spending my time. Give me the strength and courage to make the hard choices, to go where I am needed, to minister to those seemingly beyond help—to risk the company of sinners.

MY PRAYERS

_____

_____

_____

_____

_____

CORRECTION

Stern discipline awaits him who leaves the path;
he who hates correction will die.

PROVERBS 15:10 NIV

Lord, I don't enjoy being corrected, whether it comes from You or from another Christian. I'd rather believe I always do the right thing—but that isn't so. The truth is that to stay on Your narrow path, I need direction from You and wise believers.

Though I don't want to hear correcting words or experience those hard-hitting moments when I know I'm wrong, I know I need them. They seem unpleasant now, but they keep me from falling into greater error and missing Your way entirely.

Help my spirit be gentle enough to accept correction, even when it hurts. I know You only mean it for my benefit. And if I have to correct another Christian, let it be with a kind and righteous spirit.

MY PRAYERS

_____

_____

_____

_____

_____

COUNTING BLESSINGS

Enter into his gates with thanksgiving,
and into his courts with praise:
be thankful unto him, and bless his name.

PSALM 100:4

Dear Lord, what bountiful harvest I have received from You! I count blessings without number. You have given me health, a warm family life, prosperity, and a peaceful heart. You have given me strength in adversity and security in turmoil. You have given me opportunities to serve and thereby enriched my life.

I acknowledge the rich blessings that You have showered upon me. Help me appreciate them. Remove from my heart the idea that my recognition of these blessings will earn me future blessings. Let me focus on what You have done for me and rejoice in all the daily blessings You give me.

MY PRAYERS

_____

_____

_____

_____

_____

DEALING WITH GUILT

I, even I, am he that blotteth out
thy transgressions for mine own sake,
and will not remember thy sins.

ISAIAH 43:25

Sometimes, Father, I find myself striving for perfection, certain that I can live a holier life if I only work on myself a little more. Of course what happens is that I make progress on one particular sin at the expense of working on another and end up tormented by guilt.

Remind me that this is not a victory I can ever claim for myself. Sin is with me and will always be with me. Yet You promise that You will not even remember my sins, because You choose not to! You sent Your Son to deal with my sin, and the job has been done. This is not a do-it-yourself project. Thank You, Father.

MY PRAYERS

_____

_____

_____

_____

_____

DEFEATING THE ENEMY

"Behold, I give you the authority to
trample on serpents and scorpions,
and over all the power of the enemy,
and nothing shall by any means hurt you."

LUKE 10:19 NKJV

Often, I don't feel much like an overcomer, Lord. Temptation feels very real, and too often I fall into sin. But You look at my spiritual history differently. You see the long haul, both the future and the past; You see the end of my life, as well as the beginning.

You're promising me victory in the end. As I walk faithfully with You, You give me an increasing ability to say "no" to sin. The serpents of temptation fall beneath my feet and no longer harm me.

Nothing hurts me forever when I walk with You, Lord. Keep me strong in clinging to You alone.

MY PRAYERS

_____

_____

_____

_____

_____

THE END

For God so loved the world,
that he gave his only begotten Son,
that whosoever believeth
in him should not perish,
but have everlasting life.

JOHN 3:16

Father, I avoid reading movie or book reviews that go into too much detail about the plot. I enjoy the suspense of waiting to learn how the story unfolds. The ending may be happy or it may have a twist, but I want to be surprised by it.

However, in my own life, I want to know the final result. Thank You, Lord, for telling me the outcome. You have promised that if I seek You, I will find You. Jesus has already paid the penalty for my sins. A faithful life assures me that I will have an eternal home with You.

MY PRAYERS

_____

_____

_____

_____

_____

ENDURANCE

But he that shall endure unto the end,
the same shall be saved.

MATTHEW 24:13

Lord, I must admit that words like *patience* and *endurance* aren't my favorites. They make me think of gritting my teeth and bearing up under troubles—and I never look forward to troubles.

Give me Your vision of patience and endurance, Jesus. You came to earth and bore my sins, when heaven was Your rightful home. You endured much on earth so that I could relate to You. Help me see the value in patiently enduring hardship. I look forward with joy to eternity with You. Strengthen me, Lord, to be patient until that day.

MY PRAYERS

_____

_____

_____

_____

_____

EVERLASTING TRUTH

"The grass withers, and the flowers fade,
but the word of our God stands forever."

Isaiah 40:8 nlt

So much changes in life, Lord. Just when I think I'm secure, I can almost count on some fluctuation, and my world becomes different again. Just as the seasons alter and the flowers die off, life is constantly moving.

But Your truths aren't one thing in the summer season and another in fall. Your Word doesn't say one thing this month and something new ninety days later. It always shows me what You are like and never changes. I can count on Scripture always to be truthful and to lead me in the right path.

Thank You, Lord, for sharing Your everlasting truth with me. Help me to be steadfast in clinging to Your way.

My Prayers

_____

_____

_____

_____

_____

EVIDENCE

Now faith is the substance of things hoped for,
the evidence of things not seen.

HEBREWS 11:1

Lord, astronomers have recently discovered distant moons and planets they cannot see through even the strongest of telescopes. By observing the effects these bodies have on other bodies—changes in orbit, for example—they know these distant bodies simply must be there, or their effects would not be there. This is "evidence of things not seen," perhaps even the "substance of things hoped for." I admit I do not totally understand how the astronomers do this, but I find it comforting.

There is so much I do not understand about You. Still, I can see the effects of Your actions, the evidence that You are still active in my daily life and the lives of others. I do not need to physically see You to believe. Your evidence is everywhere.

MY PRAYERS

_____

_____

_____

_____

_____

FEELING FAR FROM GOD

But if from there you seek the LORD your God,
you will find him if you look for him
with all your heart and with all your soul.

DEUTERONOMY 4:29 NIV

Sometimes when I hurt, I feel so far from You, Lord, that I begin to wonder if You even care anymore. When I experience that feeling, often it's because the world has gotten in between us. I've fallen into sin, and the sin looks good. Or I've let the sand of being overly busy keep me from time with You. Forgive me, Lord.

A life off course becomes a lonely existence. Even in a crowd, I feel far from everyone. All I need to do is return to You. Turn my heart again in the right direction, Lord. Help me put aside all that divides us and draw close to Your side again.

MY PRAYERS

_____

_____

_____

_____

_____

FINDING LIFE

"Whoever finds his life will lose it,
and whoever loses his life
for my sake will find it."

MATTHEW 10:39 NIV

The new life You promise, Lord, isn't simply for a few years—not even one hundred of them. Your life lasts forever, and I will share eternity with You. That's why You tell me not to cling too closely to this world. Eternity doesn't depend on my going with the crowd here on earth, because their choices don't last. It doesn't require that I please anyone but You.

I want to use this life to make a difference for eternity. In the here and now I can share Your love with those who don't yet know You and those who struggle to live their new lives well. Whatever I lose in this world, let it be for gain in Your kingdom.

MY PRAYERS

_____

_____

_____

_____

_____

FORGIVING LOVE

"Don't tear your clothing in your grief;
instead, tear your hearts."
Return to the LORD your God,
for he is gracious and merciful.
He is not easily angered.
He is filled with kindness and
is eager not to punish you.

JOEL 2:13 NLT

When I've done wrong, it's comforting to know You want me to return to You, Lord. Though it seems right that You should hold my sin against me, that's not Your desire. You've already forgiven my sin with Jesus' sacrifice. I need simply turn to You and acknowledge my unfaithfulness.

Turn my heart from wrongdoing, Lord. I don't want to miss out on a moment of Your love and grace. Draw me close, Jesus, to Your wounded side, where I can rejoice in Your forgiving love.

MY PRAYERS

_____

_____

_____

_____

_____

THE GENUINE ARTICLE

Whatsoever things are true,
whatsoever things are honest,
whatsoever things are just,
whatsoever things are pure,
whatsoever things are lovely,
whatsoever things are of good report
. . .think on these things.

PHILIPPIANS 4:8

Father, I can see in my daily activities how people strive for easy perfection—a mathematical "proof" that solves a problem in the least number of steps, a musical composition without a discordant note, a work of art that achieves harmony and symmetric composition.

Dear Lord, I strive for a life in tune with Your orchestration. I know that to have an honorable life, I must be meticulous in eliminating the inferior elements and strive to reflect Your higher nature. I want to be a genuine Christian. I put my life in Your hands so that I can come closer to reaching that goal.

MY PRAYERS

_____

_____

_____

_____

_____

GIVING IN FAITH

But when thou makest a feast,
call the poor, the maimed, the lame, the blind:
And thou shalt be blessed;
for they cannot recompense thee:
for thou shalt be recompensed at
the resurrection of the just.

LUKE 14:13–14

Father, sometimes charity seems to be a thankless task. No one will ever repay me, and I see no immediate results to give me some sense of satisfaction. It's like dropping a penny into a bottomless well: I can't even hear it *clink* at the end of its fall.

Remind me that though the little I can give seems useless, when added to the little that millions give, my charity can make a difference. You recall every penny I drop into the alms box; the consequences of my charity are in Your hands. Help me to give in faith.

MY PRAYERS

_____

_____

_____

_____

_____

GIVING OF MYSELF

And whosoever will be chief among you,
let him be your servant:
Even as the Son of man came
not to be ministered unto, but to minister,
and to give his life a ransom for many.

MATTHEW 20:27–28

As I contemplate all the activities that demand my attention, I think of You, Jesus. You did the work of a servant by washing the feet of the apostles. Please help me remember that the greatest in the kingdom of heaven is not the one being served, but the humble one doing the serving.

Sometimes I find it easier to give from a distance than to become personally involved in situations. Help me, Lord, to fulfill the mission to serve others. I need Your strength to meet my obligations to my family, my coworkers, and members of my community.

MY PRAYERS

_____

_____

_____

_____

_____

GOD OWNS
ALL CREATION

The earth is the LORD's,
and everything in it.
The world and all its people belong to him.

PSALM 24:1 NLT

Thank You, Lord, for controlling all creation, though things can seem so confused. I often wonder where this world is going, but I'm glad I can trust in Your control over all living things.

Even people, whom You created along with the birds, bees, and other creatures, are under Your control. Though they may not all glorify You with their lives, they cannot do anything to set aside Your command of creation. Their wickedness cannot destroy Your plans for Your world.

Thank You for owning me, along with everything else. I'm incredibly glad to belong to the Lord of the universe.

MY PRAYERS

_____

_____

_____

_____

_____

GOD'S CHILDREN

*For his Holy Spirit speaks to us deep in our hearts
and tells us that we are God's children.*

ROMANS 8:16 NLT

No matter what happens to my family, Lord, Your Spirit has promised that I'm never alone. I'm always part of Your family, which may have members who get closer to my heart than some of my blood relatives. If I lost everyone You've given me—my parents, brothers, sisters, and my extended family—I'd never be alone. Thank You for caring so much for my heart that You bring me family members who love You, whether or not they're related by blood.

I'm glad to be part of Your family. Help me become a child You can be proud of, Lord.

MY PRAYERS

_____

_____

_____

_____

_____

GOD'S DIRECTION

*Trust in the L*ORD *with all thine heart;*
and lean not unto thine own understanding.
In all thy ways acknowledge him,
and he shall direct thy paths.

PROVERBS 3:5–6

I never know what the day will bring, Lord. A perfectly ordinary day may end with glory or grief, or it may end like a perfectly ordinary day usually ends. I try to prepare myself for anything that comes my way, at least mentally; but the truth is, there are too many possibilities for me to even consider. All I can do is put my trust in You and live each day in the belief that You know how everything will work out—even if I don't. You will show me which way to turn. You will guide and protect me day after day. You have a plan; and although I don't know or understand it, I trust in You.

MY PRAYERS

_____
_____
_____
_____
_____

GOD'S HONESTY

"And he who is the Glory of Israel will not lie,
nor will he change his mind,
for he is not human that
he should change his mind!"

1 SAMUEL 15:29 NLT

How glad I am, Lord, that I can trust You not to lie or change Your thinking. You follow through on every promise, and nothing ever alters Your perfection.

You want me to be honest because that's what You are; and as I grow in You, I must increasingly reflect Your nature. Help me to become completely reliable. When I tell a friend I'll help out, I want him to be able to count on me. When a coworker needs the truth, let her be able to turn to me.

Every day, make me more like You, Lord. In my own strength, I'm only human; but Your Spirit makes me ever more like You.

MY PRAYERS

_____

_____

_____

_____

_____

GOD'S JUSTICE

*"Have nothing to do with a false charge
and do not put an innocent or honest person
to death, for I will not acquit the guilty."*

EXODUS 23:7 NIV

When sin harms an innocent person, it's easy to wonder where You are, Lord. "Why did this happen?" I ask. "Why wasn't it stopped?"

Verses like this give me hope, though. You warn Your people not to do evil because You will not acquit them. How much less will You acquit someone who has no regard for You or relationship with You.

When I can't see Your justice, help me still to trust in it. Let me know a response is on its way, even if You don't show it before I meet with eternity.

MY PRAYERS

_____

_____

_____

_____

_____

GOD'S PROMISES
ARE SURE

He hath given meat unto them that fear him:
he will ever be mindful of his covenant.

PSALM 111:5

Father, being human, with human weaknesses, we may forget our promises to our children, but You never forget Your promises to us. You remain honorable and full of compassion even when we are weak and easily frightened. Your commandments stand forever, as does the redemption of Your people through Jesus Christ. Out of Your great mercy, You will always provide for those who love You and follow Your ways. Remind me of this when I am in need of food or shelter, Lord. Sometimes my needs seem to be the most important things in my life, but I know this is only panic speaking. I need never panic again: Your promises are sure. Help my desperation of today give way to Your reassurance and love.

MY PRAYERS

_____

_____

_____

_____

_____

THE GOLDEN RULE

Therefore all things whatsoever
ye would that men should do to you,
do ye even so to them:
for this is the law and the prophets.

MATTHEW 7:12

L ord, I have memorized the Bible verse that is called the Golden
Rule. Yet, putting it into practice is far more difficult than
learning the words. While You were here on earth, You demon-
strated the perfect example of living out this principle.

Jesus, I praise You for showing me compassion and granting
me forgiveness for my transgressions. Thank You for teaching me
how to have peace in my life. Lord, give me the determination to
do unto others as I want them to do unto me.

MY PRAYERS

_____

_____

_____

_____

_____

FOR GOVERNMENT LEADERS

I exhort therefore, that, first of all,
supplications, prayers, intercessions,
and giving of thanks, be made for all men;
For kings, and for all that are in authority;
that we may lead a quiet and peaceable life
in all godliness and honesty.

1 TIMOTHY 2:1–2

Heavenly Father, I ask that You guide the leaders of my country. May they have integrity, morality, and leadership ability. Guide them to extend Your influence into all areas of society. Empower them to overcome the dark forces at work in the world.

Father, I ask for Your guidance upon my government's leaders. Direct them to take our nation in the way You would have us go. Help them realize that true prosperity comes only through the application of Christian values. May the laws they make uphold and protect our right to worship You.

MY PRAYERS

_____

_____

_____

_____

GREATNESS IN SERVICE

"The greatest among you
will be your servant."

MATTHEW 23:11 NIV

It's hard to think of greatness in servanthood, Lord. Our world doesn't think that way, and breaking out of the mold takes effort. Even in church I can have a hard time seeing greatness as a matter of doing things for others.

Help me change my thinking, Jesus, and help me model the lifestyle You want every Christian to have. Instead of seeking personal fame or self-importance, I need to help others and aid them in drawing closer to You. When other people see my actions, I want them to see You.

Help me become Your servant in every way, Lord. Then I'll have the only greatness worth having—I will be distinguished in Your eyes.

MY PRAYERS

_____

_____

_____

_____

_____

HEALED BY JESUS

But he was wounded for our transgressions,
he was bruised for our iniquities:
the chastisement of our peace was upon him;
and with his stripes we are healed.

ISAIAH 53:5

Lord, I do not even know how many times You have already restored my health. I may have never seen or understood many of Your actions, and I may often credit others for what was actually Your healing and preservation. But I know You are always with me, and I thank You for Your protection.

Father God, whether it's a physical sickness or a spiritual one, You have promised I have healing in Jesus. No illness is beyond Your power, Lord. When I suffer from sin or physical pain, keep me mindful that Your hand is still on me. May each trial strengthen me spiritually and draw me nearer to You. Ultimately, I will experience Your healing—here or in heaven.

Keep me mindful of the price Your Son paid so I could enjoy a healthy relationship with You. Let my trust in You never fail.

MY PRAYERS

_____

_____

_____

_____

_____

HEART PURITY

Blessed are the pure in heart:
for they shall see God.

MATTHEW 5:8

When purity of heart, mind, and soul seems difficult, remind me of this promise, Lord. Seeing You is the greatest blessing I could receive—I especially long to look directly into Your face.

In this world, I cannot see You fully, though every day I perceive more of Your love, grace, and blessing as I draw nearer to You in obedience. I cannot see You physically, yet I get a clearer spiritual picture of You every day as I live out Your commands. Reading Your Word, praying, and acting in a way that pleases You make You ever clearer to my heart and soul.

Make my heart increasingly pure, Lord. Long before we meet face-to-face I want to know You well.

MY PRAYERS

_____

_____

_____

_____

_____

HIDDEN STRENGTH

*He gives strength to the weary
and increases the power of the weak.*

ISAIAH 40:29 NIV

I am not courageous, Lord. Like a child, sometimes I still wonder about the monsters under the bed and turn on every light in the house as soon as the sun sets. When I look at my life's challenges, I feel so small and inadequate.

Yet You promise courage and strength when I need them. Sometimes, in Your power, I even do remarkable things that cannot be explained; I can rise to great heights when necessary. After the danger is passed, my knees may give out, and I wonder how I did such wonders. Then the light dawns: You did wonders through me. Thank You for the hidden strength You give me—Your strength.

MY PRAYERS

_____

_____

_____

_____

_____

HOPE IN TROUBLE

But the needy will not always be forgotten,
nor the hope of the afflicted ever perish.

PSALM 9:18 NIV

I certainly have needs now, Lord. They overwhelm me until I hardly know where to turn.

But I still hope in You, Jesus. I know You will never forget me or desert me, and You will always provide a way out of my troubles. No matter what problems we have faced, You have never yet forgotten or given up on Your people. Though it may take some time, You faithfully respond.

In my need, assuage my physical and spiritual emptiness, Lord. To have one need fulfilled without the other will not make me complete. Without Your Spirit's flow in my life, I am still afflicted. I need Your filling, Lord.

MY PRAYERS

_____

_____

_____

_____

_____

AN INSTANT WORLD

For ye have need of patience, that,
after ye have done the will of God,
ye might receive the promise.

HEBREWS 10:36

This is an instant world, Lord. Patience is not much valued here. If I don't get what I think I need, I take charge myself and double my efforts, not even thinking about sitting back in patience and waiting for You to act. Like a little child, I run to and fro looking for something to amuse me, even when I know it's not amusement I need. Just like a child, I get myself in trouble when I run ahead of You. On days when I go off on my own, draw me close to You until I calm down and begin to think clearly. Everything is under control. All I need has been provided. All I need to contribute is faith and patience.

MY PRAYERS

_____

_____

_____

_____

_____

JESUS' FRIENDS

"You are my friends if you do what I command."

JOHN 15:14 NIV

Friendship with You, Lord, should mean the most to me. When I run out the door to be with another friend, I shouldn't leave You behind. Wherever we go, You can be a welcome third, who enjoys and blesses our fellowship.

Whatever I do, help me remember that Your friendship means more than any human relationship. I can't share with others the way I can with You; I'd never tell anyone else all the secrets of my heart. No one knows me as You do, even when I don't understand myself.

What You command, Lord, I want to do, whether I'm with others or alone. Help me and my friends to obey You always.

MY PRAYERS

_____

_____

_____

_____

_____

LABORERS WITH GOD

For we are labourers together with God:
ye are God's husbandry,
ye are God's building.

1 CORINTHIANS 3:9

The best thing about working is knowing I'm not working alone. I may plant the seeds, but You water them. I may do the weeding, but You send the sunshine. All I am and all I do is done with You, the One who created me and gifted me with whatever skills I have. You give my work—whatever type of work it may be—dignity and purpose. Your faith in me enables me to continue my duties on days when I would otherwise despair. At the end of the day my feet may be burning, but I know I am walking in Your footsteps, and that gives me peace. I thank You for the work I have. May I do it in a way that is pleasing to You and reflects Your glory.

MY PRAYERS

_____

_____

_____

_____

_____

LIGHT'S POWER

The light shines through the darkness,
and the darkness can never extinguish it.

JOHN 1:5 NLT

Your light will never be extinguished, Lord. No evil or power of Satan can overpower Your strength. No depraved man overcomes Your will. Nothing wicked conquers Your love, power, and wisdom.

Remind me of that truth when overcoming sin seems hard. Instead of thinking that I have to overcome, I must remember I have no such ability. Nothing in me pierces the darkness; only Your power pushes back Satan's murkiness and brings me into Your pure light.

Without Your light, I'm lost, Jesus. Fill me with Your brightness, and use my life to do Your work of eradicating the darkness in the world around me.

MY PRAYERS

_____

_____

_____

_____

_____

A LIVING STONE

Ye also, as lively stones,
are built up a spiritual house,
an holy priesthood,
to offer up spiritual sacrifices,
acceptable to God by Jesus Christ.

1 PETER 2:5

Lord, I am amazed at the ceaseless action of waves. I find stones that are rounded smooth by the continuous pounding of the water. Even the edges of broken glass are smoothed away until they are no longer sharp.

Father, I see Your ceaseless action on my life in the same way. Day by day, You remove my rough edges. You blunt my sharp tongue, soften my overbearing manner, cool my hot temper, and smooth out my uneven disposition. From a rough and unremarkable stone, You have made me into something better. Thank You for continuously changing me.

MY PRAYERS

_____

_____

_____

_____

_____

THE LORD DELIVERS

*The Lord knoweth how to deliver
the godly out of temptations.*

2 PETER 2:9

Self-control is not an easy path to follow. Those of us who try to follow You know it is steep, the footing insecure. Often it seems that others are standing at the edge of the path and throwing rocks under my feet, just to watch me stumble. If I lose my footing and fall, they take great pleasure in mocking me. Without Your help, I would fail to reach my goal; but You have promised that You will be there for me when I call for help. I do not know how to deliver myself from temptation, but You know the way. You have been there. You suffered temptation and won all Your trials. When I stumble, Your arms catch me; if I fall, You bring me to my feet and guide me onward.

MY PRAYERS

_____

_____

_____

_____

_____

LOVE

Know therefore that the LORD thy God,
he is God, the faithful God,
which keepeth covenant and mercy
with them that love him
and keep his commandments
to a thousand generations.

DEUTERONOMY 7:9

Omnipotent Father, there are no limitations to the amount of love and attention You can bestow upon each of Your children. Although I receive Your rich blessings all the time, day and night, I pray that I will not take Your love for granted.

Lord, the more I know You and understand You, the more I will see and appreciate Your love. I pray that I will experience You more deeply so that my love for You will increase. You have taught me that sacrifices must be made for love to grow. I submit to You. Demolish me and then rebuild me so I may be one with You.

MY PRAYERS

_____

_____

_____

_____

_____

LOVE'S COURAGE

*O love the L*ORD*, all ye his saints:*
*for the L*ORD *preserveth the faithful,*
and plentifully rewardeth the proud doer.
Be of good courage,
and he shall strengthen your heart,
*all ye that hope in the L*ORD*.*

PSALM 31:23–24

When my courage seems so small and slips away, when sin seeks to pull me from Your path, Lord, remind me of these verses. I need only trust in You, the One who keeps me safe and brings good things into my life. You reward my feeble efforts and multiply them through Your strength as I simply love You and respond to You in faith.

I want to be strong—in You and for You. Give me courage each day. When evil seems to abound and sin distracts me from Your way, thank You that Your love abounds still more.

MY PRAYERS

_____

_____

_____

_____

_____

MY REACTIONS

If ye endure chastening,
God dealeth with you as with sons;
for what son is he whom
the father chasteneth not?

HEBREWS 12:7

You are my perfect Father, but I am Your imperfect child, full of human failings and sometimes in need of correction. If You did not love me, You would ignore my misdeeds, leaving me to my own devices and letting the chips fall where they may, but You do not do this. You love me and therefore correct me, as I do with my own children.

Like my children, I do not always welcome correction. I pout; I avoid You; I try to go my own way. I even say, "It's not my fault!" as if I were not responsible for my own actions. In times like these, be patient with me, Father, because I cannot live without Your love.

MY PRAYERS

_____

_____

_____

_____

_____

NOT FORSAKEN

But I am poor and needy;
yet the Lord thinketh upon me.

PSALM 40:17

Who am I to come to You with prayers and thanksgiving, Lord? Who cares what I think? I am not a great person—not even a particularly good person. I will never do wonderful things or be loved by everyone who knows me. I will spend my life in loneliness and fear, just another nobody in a world full of nobodies.

But still You think about me. You don't just notice me and pass on—You actually take the time to think about me, to pay attention to me, to help me when I need help, and to protect me when I need protecting. I am not alone; I am not forsaken. Thank You, Lord!

MY PRAYERS

_____

_____

_____

_____

_____

NOTHING NEW

I have seen all the works
that are done under the sun;
and, behold, all is vanity
and vexation of spirit.

ECCLESIASTES 1:14

Each day, Lord, I am bombarded with advertisements. Embedded in the glittering generalities is the assurance that the merchandise is on the leading edge. The fashion models are chosen because of their appeal to the young and vigorous. I suddenly discover a product that is essential, although I have been getting along without it all of my life. I disparage as outdated my perfectly serviceable possessions.

Heavenly Father, I pray that I will not allow advertisements to exploit my tendency to be discontented. Help me dismiss sales pitches that appeal to desire and pride. Keep me away from the idea that I can improve my future with things rather than by living for You.

MY PRAYERS

_____

_____

_____

_____

_____

OUR SOURCE OF STRENGTH

The righteous also shall hold on his way,
and he that hath clean hands
shall be stronger and stronger.

JOB 17:9

On my own, I am rarely as strong as I need to be, Lord. Sickness weakens me; cares and worry tire my mind and make me less productive than I want to be. Old age will eventually defeat my body. Even when I am physically fit, I know there is weakness in me. But You promise that I will be able to continue in Your Way as long as I have faith and I trust Your promises. Make me stronger every day, Lord, no matter how heavy my burdens may be. Show me all the good You have done for the faithful throughout history, and give me some of Your strength when my own fails. Let my dependence on You turn weakness into strength.

MY PRAYERS

_____

_____

_____

_____

_____

THE PATHWAY

And thine ears shall hear
a word behind thee, saying,
This is the way, walk ye in it,
when ye turn to the right hand,
and when ye turn to the left.

ISAIAH 30:21

If life is like a pathway in the woods, I'm always making problems for myself along the way. The woods are deep and dark, and I am easily distracted. I go off to the left to find a hidden spring that I can hear bubbling up, only to lose the path. I follow the tracks of a deer until sunset and barely find shelter before darkness falls. I make the same mistakes on the path of life, losing sight of the trail and calling out for You to find me before it's too late and I am lost forever.

Thank You for finding me, Lord, for putting my feet back on the path and leading me home.

My Prayers

_____

_____

_____

_____

_____

PEACE

When a man's ways please the Lord,
he maketh even his enemies
to be at peace with him.

Proverbs 16:7

Lord, You know I want my ways to please You. Serving You is the greatest thing I can do with my life. As an added benefit, You have promised that because I obey, You will smooth my path. Even my enemies will become peaceful.

I've already seen Your promise at work in my life. Sometimes, when life seems to be getting rough, I pray—and the path becomes smooth before me. Issues I thought would become real problems turn into nothing at all, and I know You have answered my prayer.

Thank You for Your peace, which goes before me every day to bless my life.

My Prayers

_____

_____

_____

_____

_____

PERSISTENT PRAYER

"Ask, and it will be given to you;
seek, and you will find;
knock, and it will be opened to you.
For everyone who asks receives,
and he who seeks finds,
and to him who knocks it will be opened."

MATTHEW 7:7–8 NKJV

I've asked for things in prayer and not gotten them, Lord. Then I've started to wonder if I should have asked at all. But this verse encourages me not only to ask once, but to seek and knock persistently for the good things of Your kingdom.

When I don't get an immediate answer, Lord, remind me to check with You to make sure my request is good—and then to keep on trusting and persisting. You don't ignore my prayers, even if I don't get the response I'd wanted. You will answer when the time is right.

Thank You, Lord, for Your answers to every prayer.

MY PRAYERS

_____

_____

_____

_____

_____

THE PERSON WITHIN

*For man looketh on the outward appearance,
but the LORD looketh on the heart.*

1 SAMUEL 16:7

We are too conscious of outward beauty today, Lord. Our singers, our heroes, our role models —even our politicians—are expected to meet certain standards of beauty. Even worse, we instinctively trust the beautiful, never looking beyond their bodies, as though perfect hair indicates a perfect brain or a pure heart. When we stop to think about it, we know this is foolish, but we rarely do think about it. Make me more conscious of this error, Lord. Teach me to look through appearance when I choose my heroes or my spouse. A perfect hairdo should not unduly influence me—it may be warming a very small brain. An expensive Italian suit may very well be covering a dark heart. Help me see beyond beauty—or the lack of it.

MY PRAYERS

_____

_____

_____

_____

_____

A PERSONAL PRAYER

And this is life eternal,
that they might know thee the only true God,
and Jesus Christ, whom thou hast sent.

JOHN 17:3

Heavenly Father, in this prayer I want to speak to You about myself. I pray that it is not a selfish prayer, for my ultimate goal is to be right with You. Please make a way for me to avoid sin and help me to accept Your forgiveness when I do sin. I long to be right with You. Direct my steps to always be in the path of righteousness.

Father, help me recognize the work You have given me to do, and assist me as I try to glorify You. Stamp Your name on my heart so that I may live eternally in Your presence.

MY PRAYERS

_____

_____

_____

_____

_____

THE PICTURE JESUS SEES

According as he hath chosen us in him
before the foundation of the world,
that we should be holy and without blame
before him in love.

EPHESIANS 1:4

Dear Lord, with an auto-everything camera, even I can take pictures. But I have found that snapping the shutter does not guarantee a good photo. I've learned to aim the camera to cut out distracting elements such as road signs, to avoid trees growing out of heads, and to keep power lines from cutting across a scenic view. Sometimes I have to use a flash to illuminate a dark subject.

Jesus, in Your honored position of viewing earth from heaven, what kind of image of my life do You see? Remove all distracting elements from my Christian character. Illuminate me with Your love, and frame me in Your Word. I pray You will compose my life so it presents a pleasing picture to others—and to You.

MY PRAYERS

_____

_____

_____

_____

_____

PLANNING

A man's heart deviseth his way:
but the LORD directeth his steps.

PROVERBS 16:9

I have made lots of plans in my lifetime, Father, some of them just wishful thinking, some very concrete and detailed. They were all good mental discipline, but not all that many worked out the way I thought they would. Some I was not at all suited for; others would take me two lifetimes to complete. Still, it's good to have some idea of where I want to go and what I will need along the way. Not all my plans are in Your will, though—even those that sound like good ideas to me. When they are not, You show me a better idea, and I thank You for Your guidance. Keep me on the right path when my own plans are flawed, because only You know where You need me to be today and tomorrow.

MY PRAYERS

_____

_____

_____

_____

_____

POSSIBILITIES

All things are possible to him that believeth.

MARK 9:23

What an amazing promise this is, Lord! I can hardly believe You wrote this to me. You've opened so many doors to me simply because I have faith in You.

I know that amazing promise doesn't mean I can demand anything I want. There are plenty of wrong things in this world—or things that would simply be wrong for me—that Your promise doesn't automatically cover. But You have given me an open door to all the good things You offer me, all the positive things that I can do, and all the challenges You want me to overcome.

When it comes to the things You say are right, I don't want to think too small. All things are possible in You.

MY PRAYERS

_____

_____

_____

_____

_____

THE POWER
OF THE WORD

For our gospel came not unto you in word only,
but also in power, and in the Holy Ghost,
and in much assurance;
as ye know what manner of men we were
among you for your sake.

1 THESSALONIANS 1:5

Lord, I confess to You that I often read the Bible hurriedly and without much comprehension. Despite my sometimes superficial reading, I do gain something from staying in touch with You. More gratifying, though, are those occasions when I take the time to think upon Your Word and meditate upon Your message. Most useful of all are those occasions when certain passages capture my attention. For several days I carry the verses around in my thoughts and pray about them. Slowly, by continually holding them in my mind, they dawn into full light.

Father, I pray that the power of Your Word will transform my mind. Change the printed words into words written on my heart and living in my spirit.

MY PRAYERS

_____

_____

_____

_____

_____

PRAISE IN
THE ASSEMBLY

To appoint unto them that mourn in Zion,
to give unto them beauty for ashes,
the oil of joy for mourning,
the garment of praise for the spirit of heaviness
. . .that he might be glorified.

ISAIAH 61:3

Thank You, Lord, that in Your wisdom You have given me Your day as a reminder to rest and renew. As I assemble with other believers, the stresses of the week dissipate. I feel Your living Spirit as the unified body of Christ worships You.

I thank You, Lord, for allowing me to be a part of the assembly, where the cares of the week are put aside. There is joy in my heart as I leave Your house. Fellowship with other believers ignites a fire that burns in my heart throughout the week.

MY PRAYERS

_____

_____

_____

_____

_____

A PRAYER
FOR THOSE IN NEED

Blessed is he that considereth the poor:
the LORD will deliver him in time of trouble.

PSALM 41:1

Father, today I pray for those who are struggling with poverty, those in my own community and throughout the world. Let me not fall into the trap of considering the poor as different from myself, for You know how rapidly fortunes can change and the wealthiest can fall into difficulty. Help me be generous with both my donations and my efforts to help those in need. The little I can contribute seems ineffective, but You will multiply it because I am Your child and precious in Your sight.

MY PRAYERS

_____

_____

_____

_____

_____

PREJUDICE

Thou shalt not avenge, nor bear any grudge
against the children of thy people,
but thou shalt love thy neighbour as thyself:
I am the LORD.

LEVITICUS 19:18

Jesus, You have taught me that to live in heaven forever with You, I must be a good neighbor. Your parable about the Samaritan who offered aid shows that every person should be treated with kindness, even people that others might hate or despise because of their language, skin color, or place of birth.

Lord, so that I can live with You in heaven, give me the determination to act upon the truth that all people are equal in Your sight. Let me show kindness to everyone, because all are created in Your image.

MY PRAYERS

_____

_____

_____

_____

_____

PUTTING ON CHRIST'S IMAGE

You have put off the old man with his deeds,
and have put on the new man who is
renewed in knowledge according to
the image of Him who created him.

COLOSSIANS 3:9–10 NKJV

Lord, I'm being renewed, according to Your promise. As I grow in knowledge of You, I become more like You every day.

Some days I don't feel much like You, Lord, when I struggle to do Your will. But other days, I begin to see the changes You've made in my heart. I rejoice in that new me. But I ask You: Help me not to become proud about the reconstruction and give myself the credit. I know only You could make these heart alterations.

In all things make me into Your image, Lord. I need the change so much.

MY PRAYERS

_____

_____

_____

_____

_____

A READY HARVEST

Pray ye therefore the Lord of the harvest,
that he will send forth labourers
into his harvest.

MATTHEW 9:38

Father, even from my limited gardening experience, I've seen that weeds grow without encouragement, but good crops require attention. Seeds must be planted in soil that has been prepared to receive them, weeds must be eliminated, and produce must be harvested at the right time.

Almighty Savior, I see that the same sequence is necessary to produce a spiritual harvest. Lord, make me a faithful worker in Your harvest. Help me to be diligent in the work that brings the lost to You. May I have an urgency to gather souls into Your kingdom before the season is past and the crop is lost.

MY PRAYERS

_____

_____

_____

_____

_____

REAL DANGERS

Wherefore gird up the loins of your mind,
be sober, and hope to the end for the grace
that is to be brought unto you
at the revelation of Jesus Christ.

1 PETER 1:13

Sometimes danger is too real. A child becomes dangerously ill, a relative has a stroke, or someone we love is in an accident. We all react differently to such disasters, but eventually we all fall apart. Even those who seem strong as a rock shake on the inside. Somehow we manage to cope, to hold ourselves together and do what needs to be done in spite of our fear and grief. We live in hope: first in hope of a cure, then, if that fails, in hope of salvation. When all hope seems to be lost, Lord, be with those who suffer. Help them to never abandon hope, for all things are possible with You.

MY PRAYERS

_____

_____

_____

_____

_____

RESPONSIBILITY

While we look not at the things which are seen,
but at the things which are not seen:
for the things which are seen are temporal;
but the things which are not seen are eternal.

2 CORINTHIANS 4:18

Father, when I was young, some children would excuse their failures or belittle someone else's successes by saying, "In a hundred years no one will remember this." Now, that comment allows me to contrast trivial and important matters. Significant comments and actions have a way of reaching beyond the present and affecting eternity.

Lord, let me never take lightly my responsibility to dedicate my words and actions to You. Use what I say and do to influence someone to seek eternity with You in heaven. Today I trust that I have done all I could for You.

MY PRAYERS

_____

_____

_____

_____

_____

THE REWARD

Then shall thy light break forth as the morning,
and thine health shall spring forth speedily:
and thy righteousness shall go before thee;
the glory of the LORD shall be thy reward.

ISAIAH 58:8

You promise me wonderful rewards when I am charitable, Lord. I will be "like a watered garden, and like a spring of water, whose waters fail not" (Isaiah 58:11). Good health will come to me, as well as good reputation; and I will live a life of righteousness. Remind me of this the next time I pass up a charity event for an evening in front of the television set or hang up the telephone without even listening to the caller. I cannot answer every request made of me, so I count on You to guide me as to where I should invest my efforts in such a way as to bring You glory.

MY PRAYERS

_____

_____

_____

_____

_____

RIGHTEOUSNESS

The LORD openeth the eyes of the blind:
the LORD raiseth them that are bowed down:
the LORD loveth the righteous.

PSALM 146:8

Thank You, Lord God, for opening my eyes to see Your righteousness and raising me from my sin to new life in You. Without You, I would be blind and bowed down by sin. But Your love changed my life from the ground up.

On my own, I am never righteous. Certainly You could never love me for my deeds. Yet in Your generous, gracious love, You cared for me even when I ignored You.

Help me to love others as You have loved me. I want to be part of Your mission to open blind eyes and raise bowed-down hearts.

MY PRAYERS

_____

_____

_____

_____

_____

THE SALVATION OF ALL

For this is good and acceptable
in the sight of God our Saviour;
Who will have all men to be saved,
and to come unto
the knowledge of the truth.

1 TIMOTHY 2:3–4

Loving Father, only You know what is in a person's heart; only You are able to judge and save. You say it is Your desire that all should be saved and know Your truth, that through Your Son You have made salvation available to me if I but ask for it. I thank You for this greatest blessing of all.

Remind me that I am not Your gatekeeper or Your judge. My task is to spread the joyful gospel to all, to believe You will make my efforts fruitful, and never to stand in the way of another's salvation. Open my heart, show me where I am needed, and I will trust the rest to You.

MY PRAYERS

_____

_____

_____

_____

_____

A SEAT AT THE TABLE

Use hospitality one to another without grudging.

1 PETER 4:9

Hospitality involves an effort, whether it's a dinner party for twelve or throwing another potato in the stew for a child who doesn't want to eat at home that night. Hospitality means greeting newcomers after church services, maybe giving them the name of a good babysitter or pizza place. It means going to my child's piano recital and applauding every child, not just my own. It is doing little kindnesses cheerfully.

Lord, You welcomed me into Your family with love and acceptance. I was not worthy of Your hospitality, but You found me a seat at the table and fed me with Your Word. Help me be as kind to others as You have been to me—cheerfully welcoming everyone who wishes to dine with me tonight.

MY PRAYERS

_____

_____

_____

_____

_____

SELF-DISCIPLINE

For God did not give us a spirit of timidity,
but a spirit of power,
of love and of self-discipline.

2 TIMOTHY 1:7 NIV

As You grow my faith, Lord, You've made me aware that serving You shouldn't be a hit-or-miss thing—an option among others—but my life goal. Every choice I make should boldly work to forward Your kingdom, not my own self-interest.

I don't have to take that bold stance alone. Even when I lack strength to do the right thing, to make a choice that will be good for many days instead of just one, You help me decide well. When I'd like to go for the short-term benefit, Your Spirit reminds me I'm not only living for today—there's eternity to consider.

In You I have a spirit of power, love, and the self-discipline that obedience requires. Help me to live faithfully only for You, Lord.

MY PRAYERS

_____

_____

_____

_____

_____

SELF-HELP

"But the word of the LORD endures forever."
Now this is the word
which by the gospel was preached to you.

1 PETER 1:25 NKJV

Father, around the office I see people carrying self-help books to read during their lunch breaks. Each month another title makes the bestseller list. Yet, few have enough substance to be enduring classics.

Lord, when I study my human nature, I find many constants in my character—I am sinful, selfish, full of pride, sometimes afraid, and always facing death. The Bible addresses all these issues. Your Word is more thorough than any contemporary book that would try to show me how to improve myself without Your assistance. May I always remember to turn to Your enduring guidebook for daily living and eternal salvation.

MY PRAYERS

_____

_____

_____

_____

_____

SHARING

And God will generously provide all you need.
Then you will always have everything you need
and plenty left over to share with others.

2 CORINTHIANS 9:8 NLT

Lord, You've given me so much. Thank You for the generous way You've cared for all my needs. Though I may not always have a lot of extra money in the bank, my true necessities are always covered. And I'm continually rich in Your blessings.

Whatever I do have, Lord, help me share abundantly with others. I know that when I give out of what You've blessed me with, You always replenish my store. Whether my need is cash, food, or a place to live, I can trust in Your faithfulness every day.

Thank You for being ever faithful, Father. Your generosity blesses my life.

MY PRAYERS

_____

_____

_____

_____

_____

SIN FORGIVEN

"Blessed is the man whose sin
the Lord will never count against him."

Romans 4:8 NIV

Before I knew You, Lord, I could not understand the blessings of forgiven sin. But Your Spirit's cleansing and the freedom that followed faith are more wonderful than I could ever have imagined. Nothing the world offers can take their place.

Thank You for not counting my sin against me, but instead sending Your Son to take my place on the cross. If You'd left me to pay the price for my own wrongs, new life would have been impossible. But because You've put my sin away from me, everything's changed. Your pardon affects every corner of my being.

I'm totally blessed by Your forgiveness, Lord. Thank You from the bottom of my soul.

My Prayers

_____

_____

_____

_____

_____

A SONG OF PRAISE

The LORD is my strength and my shield;
my heart trusted in him, and I am helped:
therefore my heart greatly rejoiceth;
and with my song will I praise him.

PSALM 28:7

I sing to You, O Lord, a continual song of praise. I declare Your name to all those who come into my presence. Words of thanksgiving are forever upon my lips. I can sing a new song because of Your grace and power. Your holy name is exalted in heaven and on earth, O Lord Most High. Your righteousness causes my heart to rejoice and break forth in a song of praise: "Glory to the God of my salvation. The generosity of Your compassion overwhelms my soul."

MY PRAYERS

_____

_____

_____

_____

_____

STEADFAST FAITH

"Therefore I say to you,
whatever things you ask when you pray,
believe that you receive them,
and you will have them."

MARK 11:24 NKJV

I'm so glad that all I have to do is believe, and I can receive the best from Your hand, Lord. But sometimes that believing is harder than it sounds. So many things—even good ones—can slide between my belief and the words I speak. Doubts often come to me more easily than faith.

On my own, I'm not very good at trusting You when life turns black. I tend to forget this verse or doubt that it's really for me. That's when I need to realize that my eyes are on the wrong thing—this world—when they should be on You.

Keep me steadfastly looking at You, Lord. Then I'll have all I could ask for.

MY PRAYERS

_____

_____

_____

_____

_____

SUFFERING

"Do not fear any of those things
which you are about to suffer.
Indeed, the devil is about to throw
some of you into prison,
that you may be tested,
and you will have tribulation ten days.
Be faithful until death,
and I will give you the crown of life."

REVELATION 2:10 NKJV

Not fearing suffering seems impossible, Lord. Suffering is not something any Christian looks forward to, yet all of us experience it in some way. Still, I know You have brought faithful believers through much more than I've experienced.

I haven't been imprisoned for my faith, Lord; but You promise You'll be there even if that should happen. Then if I stay faithful for a short time, I'll receive Your eternal crown of life and rejoice with You in heaven.

No matter what I suffer, keep me faithful to You, Jesus. I don't want anything to harm our relationship.

MY PRAYERS

_____

_____

_____

_____

_____

TEACHING ABOUT JESUS

These are the things that ye shall do;
Speak ye every man the truth
to his neighbour;
execute the judgment of truth
and peace in your gates.

ZECHARIAH 8:16

Lord Jesus, I occasionally take on the role of teacher, although I often feel inadequate for the task. My goal is to be a mentor, guide, and advisor. May I grow in knowledge, wisdom, character, and confidence so I can help those I teach to choose the proper path.

Heavenly Teacher, provide me with the ability to instill in my students a love for learning more about You, reading the Bible, talking to You in prayer, and living a life in keeping with Your Word. May I have an influence that will last a lifetime.

MY PRAYERS

_____

_____

_____

_____

_____

TONGUE FOLLOWS HEART

Before a word is on my tongue
you know it completely, O LORD.

PSALM 139:4 NIV

I can't keep a secret from You, Lord, because every word I speak is part of an open book. Before a syllable falls off my tongue, You know my thoughts and emotions. Words can't consistently hide feelings; eventually they'll directly reflect my heart and soul. In a sentence that shows what I really feel, truth finally comes out.

When I follow You closely, I need not worry. My words glorify You. Yet when I stray from You, my language changes, and people observe the alteration in my heart. Only if my heart is Yours will my words be, too, Lord. May both constantly focus on You.

MY PRAYERS

_____

_____

_____

_____

_____

UNEARNED GRACE

And I will have mercy upon her
that had not obtained mercy;
and I will say to them
which were not my people,
Thou art my people;
and they shall say, Thou art my God.

HOSEA 2:23

O Lord, how great is Your mercy to me. You owed me nothing because I paid You no heed, yet You called me. When I walked far from You, You called me to turn to Your path.

Thank You for caring for me when I wallowed in sin. I did nothing to earn Your grace, yet You gave it to me anyway. May Your great mercy be reflected in my life as I pass on mercy to those who sin against me. May mercy flow freely in my life.

MY PRAYERS

_____

_____

_____

_____

_____

UNFAILING LOVE

Love never fails.

1 CORINTHIANS 13:8 NKJV

I couldn't call my love for others "unfailing," Lord. When people irritate me, it's so easy to make unloving choices. Though I want to draw others to You by my own faithfulness, my own sin gets in the way; and I find myself being a traitor to Your kingdom.

Though my caring ability fails often, I know from experience and Your Word that Yours never does. I'm incredibly glad of this promise because I know how much I need Your love every moment of my life. If You failed to shower me with Your affection, my days would really be a mess.

Fill me with Your unfailing love for both those I relate to easily and those who are a challenge just to be with. Love them through me with Your unending compassion.

MY PRAYERS

_____

_____

_____

_____

_____

UNWORTHINESS

If we confess our sins,
he is faithful and just to forgive us our sins,
and to cleanse us from all unrighteousness.

1 JOHN 1:9

On my worst days I feel totally unworthy. I gather up my little pile of sins like dirty laundry and shake them toward the sky. "How can You possibly forgive this sin?" I ask, repeating the process until all my sins have been displayed. On my best days I calmly confess my sins (the exact same sins I had the day before), accept Your forgiveness, and go on with my life without guilt. I suspect that both reactions to guilt are acceptable, however. Confession is confession no matter how I phrase it. You have promised to cleanse me from all unrighteousness, to wipe away my guilt and make me whole if I confess my sins, and I thank You on both my good and bad days.

MY PRAYERS

_____

_____

_____

_____

_____

VALUED BY GOD

"And the very hairs on your head
are all numbered.
So don't be afraid;
you are more valuable to him than
a whole flock of sparrows."

LUKE 12:7 NLT

Sparrows aren't very important, Lord, yet You take care of even these small birds. Though some people may think them a nuisance, You know when each one falls.

Maybe it's not a huge compliment to be compared to sparrows, but I get Your message loud and clear. Everything about me, even down to how many hairs are on my head, is important to You. If You care about the birds, how much more important am I to You.

Thank You for having compassion even about the tiny things in my life. With that kind of concern, You're teaching me that I don't have to worry about a thing.

MY PRAYERS

_____

_____

_____

_____

_____

VICTORY

Therefore, my beloved brethren,
be ye stedfast, unmoveable,
always abounding in the work of the Lord,
forasmuch as ye know that your labour
is not in vain in the Lord.

1 CORINTHIANS 15:58

In my daily work, I rarely experience victory. I clean up one mess and move on to the next, knowing even greater messes are just around the corner. I never really seem to get anywhere, to win any battles, or see anything truly completed. There are precious few victories in my work. But You encourage me to hang in there and keep on working for You, because You have already won the victory in the most important battle of all—the battle for my soul. My daily problems come and go, yet if I remain steadfast and dedicated, doing the work You have given me to do, I am confident that my reward awaits me. Thank You, Lord.

MY PRAYERS

_____

_____

_____

_____

_____

WALKING IN WISDOM

And he will teach us of his ways,
and we will walk in his paths.

ISAIAH 2:3

You have promised me that I can know Your ways and walk in them, Lord. What a blessing that is to me, for I cannot know You more closely unless I know how You want me to live and can follow in Your footsteps.

I may not always be sure of my path. But I can be sure of You; as I continue to seek Your way, You will lead me to the right goal.

You, Lord Jesus, are always my goal. You are the end of my path; my eternal reward is to live with You forever. Thank You that my way leads to Your eternal home.

MY PRAYERS

_____

_____

_____

_____

_____

WALKING WITH GOD

Noah was a just man
and perfect in his generations,
and Noah walked with God.

GENESIS 6:9

Lord, I am defined by whom I choose as my heroes and whom I pattern my life after. Others interpret my character by those with whom I walk. I want to be like the heroes of old, those people of renown in the Old Testament who were described as having "walked with God."

Dear Father, give me the determination to walk at Your side. I seek an honorable walk that shows Your power and character. I know that I am not walking alone; You are with me. I have victory over impossible circumstances because I have placed myself in Your footsteps.

MY PRAYERS

_____

_____

_____

_____

_____

WASTING TIME

Favour is deceitful, and beauty is vain:
but a woman that feareth the LORD,
she shall be praised.

PROVERBS 31:30

I know friends come and go, whether they are rich and powerful or just ordinary people. Currying favor with the "right people" is rarely worth the trouble. They have nothing I want and will soon move on to other friends because I have nothing they want. Seeking personal beauty is likewise a waste of time. I may be able to hide the toll of time for a little while, but eventually the wrinkles will prevail. Help me invest my precious time in more worthy pursuits, Lord, ones that will provide lasting satisfaction. I'm not sure what You will ask of me, but I am willing to try anything You recommend and give any resulting praise to You, where it belongs.

MY PRAYERS

_____

_____

_____

_____

_____

WISDOM
AGAINST STRIFE

Mockers stir up a city,
but wise men turn away anger.

PROVERBS 29:8 NIV

Plenty of people can tear down, but building up a leader so that problems can be solved is a better solution, Lord. I recognize that. Yet I've found it easy enough to criticize or condemn a boss, a politician, or a church leader.

Instead of rushing to attack a person or a situation, I want to become a problem solver—one who turns to You for the right, peaceful solution. So move my heart far from anger and hurt, and give me Your peace to share with others. Help me not to mock them, but to turn aside anger and find a real solution. Then I know I'll be doing Your will.

MY PRAYERS

_____

_____

_____

_____

_____

WITHOUT WAVERING

Let us hold fast the profession of
our faith without wavering;
(for he is faithful that promised).

HEBREWS 10:23

Lord, with Your blood You wiped away my sins, leaving me promises to enjoy in faith until You come back again to claim me as Your own. It takes patience to live in faith, and I confess that sometimes my patience runs thin. I wonder why You don't act in ways that I can see and understand. Why is there so much evil and suffering in this world that discourage both the faithful and the unfaithful? I don't understand. Help me realize that my understanding is not necessary for the completion of Your plan. You understand everything; all I need to do is have faith. In the meantime, keep me free from wavering, Lord. Your faithfulness is perfect, and Your will will be done.

MY PRAYERS

_____

_____

_____

_____

_____

THE WORK
OF OUR HANDS

And let the beauty of
the LORD our God be upon us:
and establish thou the work
of our hands upon us;
yea, the work of our hands establish thou it.

PSALM 90:17

What I do for a living can be either secular or sacred. The choice is mine. The kind of work I do is not important. I can do anything in a way that glorifies You, Father. A worker in the humblest of jobs is just as capable of demonstrating Your beauty as one in the most exalted of positions. The next time I am feeling unproductive or unappreciated, remind me that I am working for Your glory, not my own. A tiny bit of Your beauty is reflected in my work, whatever it might be. May those I work with always see You in my life and be brought closer to You through me.

MY PRAYERS

_____

_____

_____

_____

_____

WORLDLY POSSESSIONS

But thou shalt remember the L<small>ORD</small> *thy God:*
for it is he that giveth thee
power to get wealth,
that he may establish his covenant
which he sware unto thy fathers,
as it is this day.

D<small>EUTERONOMY</small> 8:18

I don't think of what I have as wealth, Lord; it isn't enough to buy out a major corporation. But You've given me enough to fulfill Your covenant. You've cared for me every day of my life. I haven't appreciated enough how You've taken care of me or the way You have kept me going, even in rough times.

You've also given me countless spiritual blessings: a church to worship in, Christian friends, and Your love.

Thank You for the spiritual and financial wealth You've given me. I want to use it to Your glory. Show me how to spend it for You this day.

M<small>Y</small> P<small>RAYERS</small>

_____

_____

_____

_____

_____

WORRY

Therefore take no thought, saying,
What shall we eat? or, What shall we drink? or,
Wherewithal shall we be clothed?
. . .for your heavenly Father knoweth that
ye have need of all these things.

MATTHEW 6:31–32

Worry is our most useless emotion. It is unproductive and dangerous. Sometimes it may prod me into taking action to save myself, but even then there is no guarantee that my actions will be effective because I do not think rationally when I am consumed with worry. Most of the time, worry disables me, locks me in my room, separates me from those who would be willing to help. It convinces me that I am unworthy, or stupid, or unforgiven—all lies of the devil, not Your judgments. Being concerned about my future is one thing; letting worry cripple me is a lack of faith. You know what I need, Lord, and You will provide.

MY PRAYERS

_____

_____

_____

_____

_____

WRONG IDEAS

As the Scriptures say,
"I will destroy human wisdom and
discard their most brilliant ideas."

1 CORINTHIANS 1:19 NLT

You know how much we treasure our ideas, Lord. The things we think—the beliefs we hold—are precious to us. But You promise us that human ideas are limited, and even our most brilliant ones pale compared to Your power.

When other people's bright ideas would hurt me, I'm glad You're still in control. It's comforting to know that nothing gets past You or is beyond Your control. But help me to remember that Your power also limits my human wisdom. When I think I'm being the smartest, my idea could be valueless if it doesn't side with Your wisdom.

Keep me in Your wise ways, Lord. I don't want my best ideas discarded because they were dead wrong.

MY PRAYERS

_____

_____

_____

_____

_____